LOVE IS A FLAME OF THE LORD

More Homilies on the Just Word

WALTER J. BURGHARDT, S.J.

PAULIST PRESS
New York/Mahwah, N.J.

also by Walter J. Burghardt, S.J.
published by Paulist Press

GRACE ON CRUTCHES
LOVELY IN EYES NOT HIS
PREACHING: THE ART AND THE CRAFT
SEASONS THAT LAUGH OR WEEP
SIR, WE WOULD LIKE TO SEE JESUS
STILL PROCLAIMING YOUR WONDERS
TELL THE NEXT GENERATION
TO CHRIST I LOOK
DARE TO BE CHRIST
WHEN CHRIST MEETS CHRIST
SPEAK THE WORD WITH BOLDNESS

Illustrations by John Gummere

Copyright © 1995 by the New York Province of the Society of Jesus

Library of Congress Cataloging-in-Publication Data

Burghardt, Walter J.
    Love is a flame of the Lord : more homilies on the just Word / Walter J. Burghardt.
        p.   cm.
    Includes bibliographical references.
    ISBN 0-8091-3603-1 (alk. paper)
    1. Catholic Church—Sermons. 2. Sermons, American. 3. Christianity and justice—Catholic Church—Sermons. 4. Jesus Christ—Seven last words—Sermons. I. Title.
BX1756.B828L67 1995   95-22767
252'.02,—dc20   CIP

Published by Paulist Press
997 Macarthur Boulevard
Mahwah, NJ 07430

Printed and bound in the
United States of America

TABLE OF CONTENTS

ORDINARY TIME

WEDDING HOMILIES

MEDLEY

PREFACE

In several ways the present set of homilies continues an approach to preaching apparent in the more recent of my collections which the Paulist Press has graciously presented to the public. First, there is an ongoing struggle with Scripture. Not satisfied with bare quotations, for all the undoubted power of the biblical Word. With that, a twin struggle: What did the text mean then, and what might it be saying now? Second, a relentless effort to confront contemporary living, today's moral and religious issues, today's cultural movements, not so much with ethical justice (give each what each deserves) as with biblical justice. I mean fidelity to relationships, to responsibilities, that stem from a covenant. Three sets of such responsibilities cover the gamut of human living: (1) Love God above all else. (1) Treat every man, woman, and child like another self. (3) Touch the earth, the nonhuman, with unfailing reverence.

Still, in at least two ways the present collection differs from the preceding. For the first time, I am presenting sermons on the Seven Last Words of Jesus—an extraordinary homiletic experience in Seattle's St. James Cathedral on Good Friday 1994. And in the homilies for Ordinary Time, nine of the 13 are weekday presentations. These had two advantages: They challenged me to address myself to a number of liturgical readings not usually presented on Sundays, and I was challenging priests and other preachers who had come together to participate in my project, Preaching the Just Word. How preach effectively on justice issues when the very word "justice" conjures up images that inflame the pews: wastrels on welfare, lazy folk misusing our hard-earned money? Believe me, I face the problem week after week.

An optimistic note: I continue to be delighted, and grateful to God, for the number of laity and priests of all ages and conditions who find meditation on my homilies a profound source of personal and communal spirituality. Increasingly I realize that, no matter how seriously I sow the biblical Word, it is always God who gives the increase.

My title stems from an intriguing potential interpretation of the Song of Songs 8:6. There the fiery quality of love is said to be "a flame of *yah*." Usually explained as "a Yahweh flame" of high burning intensity, it "could mean that the fire of love is a fire of Yahweh, a participation in the Lord's white-hot love" (Roland E. Murphy, O.Carm., in *The New Jerome Biblical Commentary*, p. 465). So I prefer to understand it.

Walter J. Burghardt, S.J.
January 1, 1995

FROM
ADVENT
TO
EPIPHANY

1
HEAD TRIP OR HEART THRILL?
Third Sunday of Advent (B)

- Isaiah 61:1-2, 10-11
- 1 Thessalonians 5:16-24
- John 1:6-8, 19-28

Some decades back, a French novelist, Georges Bernanos, put on the lips of one of his characters a stinging challenge: "You say you are a Christian. Then where the devil is your joy?"

The question did not disappear with Bernanos's death in 1948. Last year, *Forbes* magazine called its 75th anniversary issue "Why We Feel So Bad When We Have It So Good." One of the articles was authored by Peggy Noonan, writer (you may recall) for Ronald Reagan, George Bush, and Dan Rather. Ms. Noonan suggested that on the whole we Americans are a terribly sad people. So many Americans (Christians not excluded) have come to expect happiness; so many are convinced that this world is their only chance to be happy; and when the world does not give them a good measure of its riches, they despair.

More pungently, take our own back yard. A frightening report: Many of Washington's children are planning their own funerals: how they want to look, how be dressed, where be waked. For they do not believe they will be around very long, do not expect to grow up. Where they play, coke and crack are homicidal kings. In the past five years, 224 of their childhood friends have died from gunfire—some deliberate targets, others just bystanders, at least one lying in a cradle. And so the living little ones have begun planning for the worst, as if their own murders are inevitable, as if their dreams will surely be just as cruelly cut short.[1] Children....

Today's liturgy, Gaudete Sunday, the Sunday to rejoice, confronts the problem head on. The opening prayer hit the nail on the head: "Lord God, may we your people, who look forward to the birthday of Christ, experience the joy of salvation." Three powerful words there:

salvation...joy...experience. Bear with Burghardt as he struggles with each word...for you.

I

Let me start with joy. For joyful reading this Advent, sacrifice today's best sellers: Tom Clancy and John Grisham, Dick Francis and Ken Follett; postpone Rush Limbaugh's *See, I Told You So*, even Howard Stern's titillating title *Private Parts*. Instead, read the four Gospels at leisure. Why? To find out where the Gospels locate joy, where God's inspired Word tells us to look for joy. Make this your personal Christmas shopping, your gift to yourself.

First, in the Gospels joy is linked with *life*, especially new life. An angel promises joy in the birth of the Baptist. When John is born, Elizabeth's neighbors rejoice with her. Pregnant Mary rejoices in God her Savior. The birth of Jesus is "good news of a great joy" (Lk 2:10). A mother no longer remembers her anguish "for joy that a [child] is born into the world" (Jn 16:21). The father of the prodigal son calls for rejoicing because "this my son was dead and is alive again" (Lk 15:24). Life....

Second, in the Gospels joy is linked with *discovery*. There is the man who "hears [God's] word and immediately receives it with joy" (Mt 13:20); the man who finds a treasure and with joy sells all to buy it; the shepherd who rejoices when he finds a straying sheep. There is the joy of the woman discovering a lost coin; the joy of the 72 disciples discovering that demons are subject to them; the joy of Jesus because the childlike have discovered their God. There is the father of the prodigal summoning his elder son to joy "because your brother was lost and has been found" (Lk 15:32). Discovery....

Third, in the Gospels joy is linked, strangely, with *suffering*. The disciples are to rejoice when slandered and persecuted. When hated and outlawed for Jesus' sake, they are to "leap for joy" (Lk 6:23). And when Jesus' disciples are told to take up their cross every day, surely they are to do so with joy in their hearts. Suffering....

Fourth, in the Gospels joy is linked with *Jesus*, the fulness of joy. John the Baptist's joy is "complete" because, as "the bridegroom's best man," he prepares Israel for Jesus. Only if the disciples abide in Jesus' love, only if what they ask they ask in Jesus' name, will their "joy be complete" (Jn 16:24). When they see Jesus again, it will bring a joy no human will take from them. And so it proves after his rising from the dead—for the disciples and for Magdalene. Why, in Jesus' risen presence the disciples are so joyful they can hardly believe what they see. Jesus....[2]

II

All this returns us to our opening prayer: "May we, your people, who look forward to the birthday of Christ, experience the joy of salvation." The joy of *salvation*. Terribly abstract, isn't it? How in God's name can you leap for joy over...salvation? But the liturgy is not concerned with abstractions, with ideas floating somewhere in mid-air. Bring it down to earth. Salvation is what we have just uncovered in the Gospels: Salvation is Jesus, is discovery, is life, is suffering.

Salvation is *Jesus*. For salvation is God's unique Son taking my flesh...for me. Salvation is a stable in a little town in the Middle East, a baby lying helpless in a feeding trough...for me. Salvation is a God-man feeding at a mother's breast...for me. Salvation is the boy Jesus learning from Joseph how to shape a plow, learning from Mary how to love God...for me. Salvation is the man Jesus hungry, weary, lonely...for me. Salvation is God's Son sold for silver and crowned with thorns, whipped like a dog and pinned to a tree...for me. Salvation, very simply, is St. Paul's exclamation, "He loved me and gave himself...for me" (Gal 2:20).

Salvation is *discovery*. For salvation is finding Christ at work, as St. Ignatius said, like a laborer in every creature he has ever fashioned—working in the billions of stars to which Christ gives *being*, in the four thousand varieties of roses to which he gives *life*, in the long-haired Labrador to which he gives *senses*, in that mind of yours to which he gives *intelligence*, in that heart of yours into which he infuses *love*. Salvation is Christ, not on a majestic throne in heaven but everywhere...in every nook and cranny of this universe. Alive not only yesterday but each moment of each creature's existence. Yes, the world is charged with the presence of Christ, with the labor of Christ. For me.

Salvation is *life*. For salvation is three divine Persons alive in me, active in me, energizing me. Salvation is new life, a new creation, through repentance, reform, God murmuring to me, "I forgive you; go in peace." Salvation is the Bread of Life—Jesus, body and blood, soul and divinity—in the palm of my hand, on the edge of my tongue, deep within my flesh. Salvation is the life within your family—what the early Christians called "a little church," with Christ the unseen guest. Salvation is the life within this community, loving one another, loving your less fortunate sisters and brothers as Jesus loves you.

And yes, salvation is a *cross*, many a cross, the cross erected (theologian Karl Rahner said) over history, over you and me. For salvation is following in the footsteps of Christ, wherever he may lead. Salvation is a journey to Jerusalem, and the road is rough, pebbled with pain, twisting and turning where we never expected. Yet even here, especially here, we touch salvation; for it is in dying that the Christian rises to new Christlife—dying to sin, dying to self, dying the numberless deaths that dot a human life, all the loves God tears from us as the years move on.

Very simply, salvation is now, every moment you and I live.

III

Now such is the salvation we pray to enjoy. But our opening prayer is not satisfied to exclaim that salvation is a joyful reality. We ask to *experience* that joy. For all too long, the word "experience" was a no-no within Catholicism. It was associated with Protestantism; it had overtones of the Modernist "heresy" that troubled the Church early in this century. It seemed to play down reason, the rational side of our nature, gave far too much play to our emotions and our passions, to fear and anger, to delight and love, to grief and despair, to agony and ecstasy.

No, good friends, the God-man who cried at his mother's breast, who felt the pangs of hunger in his stomach, who sweated blood out of raging fear, who twisted on a cross for us did not experience all this simply so that we might live a Christian "head trip." I mean, accept God's revelation to us in Christ with a cool act of faith: I do believe that there is one God in three divine Persons; that Jesus is both divine and human; that the Eucharistic Christ is really present, body and blood, soul and divinity, on the altar, in the tabernacle, and in my body; that life doesn't end at 40 or at death, but there is endless life on the other side of the grave. What Advent asks of God is that we *experience* the story of our salvation. The same passion that inflames a million Redskin rooters (or used to) should lay hold of my blood and bones when I look at Jesus twitching helplessly in Bethlehem and rising gloriously from the rock—for me.

Thank God I can exult with angels on Christmas and cry with Magdalene on Good Friday. Thank God my flesh crawls when I remember what my sins did to Christ, and my skin makes music when I listen to Handel's *Messiah*. Thank God I shiver in wonder when I sense Father, Son, and Spirit shaping this fragile skin-and-bones into a new creature alive with God's own life. Thank God I can share a perceptive nun's experience versified under the title "Discovery":

> It's this that makes
>   My spirit spin,
> My bones to quake,
>   My blood run thin,
> My flesh to melt
>   Inside my skin,

> My very pulse
>> Create a din—
> It's this that makes
>> My spirit spin:
> That Heaven is
>> Not *up*, but *in!*[3]

What is happening here is a genuine encounter with God. This is what a remarkable philosopher, Jacques Maritain, meant when he insisted that the high point of knowledge is not a brilliant idea; it's an experience: I *feel* God. This, we are told on good theological authority, is not reserved for mystics; this is what God's grace wants to do for each and all of us. It is something like this that God promised through the prophet Jeremiah to the Israelites exiled to Babylon—promises to you and me:

> ...I know the plans I have for you,...plans for your welfare and not for harm, to give you a future with hope. Then when you call upon me and come and pray to me, I will hear you. When you search for me, you will find me; if you seek me with all your heart, I will let you find me....
>
> (Jer 29:11-14)

Yes indeed, let's pray for an Advent grace beyond compare—perhaps address our prayer to her who first held this infant in her arms. "Mother of Jesus and my mother too, help me to *experience* the joy of your Son's birth. Not just another head trip, an orthodox realization in my mind that he took my flesh to make me one with him. Let this realization flood my whole being, take possession of all my senses, excite me, thrill me. Let this Advent be a discovery. Let me discover your Son somewhat as you discovered him in Bethlehem. Not words about him but Jesus himself, wearing my flesh, my Lord and my God yes, but still wonderfully human, approachable, loving and lovable, caring. When he touches my hand, my tongue, my heart in the Eucharist, open my whole person to experience his coming, not to a crib but to me. Let me not experience bread; let me see your Son's smile, hear the beauty of his voice, touch his glorified wounds, taste the sweetness of the Lord. Even with death all around me, the violence that saddens my existence, let me experience the joy of being alive in Christ." Alive in Christ.

Holy Trinity Church
Washington, D.C.
December 12, 1993

2
LITTLE CHRIST, LITTLE CHILDREN
Epiphany Week, Monday (B)

- 1 John 3:22—4:6
- Matthew 4:12-17, 23-25

Strangely, my homily this evening stems from a single Greek word in John's first letter: *teknía*. It's a diminutive of the Greek word for "children," and so it means "little children"—actually little or affectionately little. Jesus used it in familiar, loving address to his disciples. You remember his words at the Last Supper, once Judas had gone out into the night: "Little children, I am with you only a little longer" (Jn 13:33). John used it when writing to his spiritual children: "Little children, let us love, not [only] in word or speech, but in truth and action" (1 Jn 3:18).

In this week called Epiphany, I find the word particularly pertinent. In three contexts: (1) yesterday's Magi, (2) everyday's Christian, (3) today's children. A word on each.

I

First, yesterday's Magi. Remarkable men, these three strangers from the East. Not only because they were in all probability astrologers or astronomers, people who studied the movement of the stars as a guide to major events. This was indeed important; if they had not followed their star, how would they ever have reached Bethlehem?[1] But even more importantly, they were looking for a child. Recall the question they asked in Jerusalem: "Where is the child who has been born king of the Jews? For we observed his star at its rising, and have come to pay him homage" (Mt 2:2). And Matthew tells us, when "they saw the child with Mary his mother, they knelt down and paid him homage" (v. 11).[2]

In the mind of Matthew, these Gentile Magi who yearned so sincerely to pay homage to the king of the Jews were a striking contrast to the Herod who claimed to be king of the Jews and pretended to pay homage to the child. I try to imagine what feelings suffused those starry-eyed Magi before a little child. A child in a feeding trough, with animals for companions.[3] Reverence indeed, submission, prostration before a king. But surely not a cold head trip. Not in the presence of an infant. Not after a laborious trip from Persia or Babylon, from Arabia or the Syrian Desert. Surely different from the homage they paid to King Herod; surely feelings of profound love. In fact, Matthew's language suggests the attitude a man or woman should have in the presence of God.

Simply, in Matthew's theology the Magi prefigure those Gentiles who were part of Matthew's community. Reverence and love for a child, a unique child, God's Son in our flesh.

II

But the Magi prefigure not only *Matthew's* community; they foreshadow the whole community of Christians—foreshadow you and me. For we are those whom Jesus addresses as *teknía*, little children—addresses familiarly, lovingly. Why? Because we too have seen a star, have seen a child. Not the way the Magi saw star and child—with the eyes of the flesh. As the Second Epistle of Peter puts it, "Although you have not seen him, you love him; and even though you do not see him now, you believe in him and rejoice with an indescribable and glorious joy, for you are receiving the outcome of your faith, the salvation of your souls" (1 Pet 1:8-9).

That is why "little children" runs like a refrain through John's letter. "My little children, I am writing these things to you so that you may not sin" (1 Jn 2:1). "I am writing to you, little children, because your sins are forgiven" (2:12). "And now, little children, abide in [Jesus]" (2:28). "Little children, let no one deceive you" (3:7). "Little children, let us love, not [only] in word or speech, but in truth and action" (3:18). "Little children, you are from God" (4:4). "Little children, keep yourselves from idols" (5:21). His disciples are his children because they are children of God: "they have been born of God" (3:9).

Ultimately, we are little children because we are children of God, because we are brothers and sisters of Jesus. Not poetic license. St. Paul put it with crystal clarity to the Christians of Rome: "All who are led by the Spirit of God are children of God. For you did not receive a spirit of slavery to fall back into fear, but you have received a spirit of adoption, by which we cry 'Abba!/Father!' The Spirit itself bears witness with our spirit that we are children of God" (Rom 8:14-16).

III

Third, the little children are today's young.[4] Unfortunately, all too many of them are heirs of the innocents in Bethlehem, whom Herod slew because any one of them might have been the child Jesus. These are not abstractions.

"If the well-being of its children is the proper measure of the health of a civilization," *Fortune* magazine tells us, "the United States is in grave danger."[5] One of every five children grows up in poverty. Every day more than three children die of injuries inflicted by abusive parents. Every day some 1.3 million latchkey kids 5 to 14 return to empty homes to fend for themselves. Every day more than 2,200 youngsters drop out of school. Every day over 500 children 10 to 14 begin to use illegal drugs, over a thousand start drinking alcohol. Each day over 1,400 teenage girls, two thirds of them unmarried, become mothers. Among 15- to 19-year olds, death by firearms is the third-leading cause of death for whites, the leading cause for blacks. 41% of boys and 24% of girls can get a gun on a whim.[6] In Washington, D.C., children are preparing their own funerals—what clothes they will wear, how they will look. Why? Because they do not expect to live very long. Hundreds of their playmates have been done to death by gunfire; no reason to think the living will be alive much longer.

You know, in our country you can get greater tax breaks for breeding horses than for bearing children.

Why this litany of disasters? Because we who are privileged to preach the gospel of Jesus Christ will not preach the Epiphany if we do not preach passionately the plight of our children. For Epiphany celebrates God manifesting, revealing, Godself in Christ to every man, woman, and child. To every child. Revealing God as a child.

But our God will hardly be manifest to children if they are hungry, neglected, sexually abused; if their minds and bodies are destroyed by coke and crack; if they are gunned down in the streets; if their source of pride, their hope, lies in a deadly weapon; if babies keep bearing babies. If each year 1.6 million images of the Christ child are prevented from ever resting in a crib or a feeding trough. If we do not allow these children to come to Christ—these children of whom Jesus said, "To such as these the kingdom of heaven belongs" (Mt 19:14).

Not our calling to *solve* complex social issues from a pulpit. But yes, our calling is to raise consciousness, to persuade our believing, faith-full people that these children are not the wards of government, that action for the little ones of Christ is not a sheerly secular occupation, that in this we are simply living the second great commandment of the law and the gospel, "You shall love your [sisters and brothers] as yourself," the commandment Jesus said "is like" loving God (Mt 22:39).

A short short story told me by John Carr of the United States Catholic Conference tells it all. A puzzled Catholic asked, "Why do we engage in all this action for the poor, the disadvantaged, the marginalized? Most of them aren't even Catholic." The response: "We do it not because *they* are Catholic, but because *we* are Catholic." The respondent? Cardinal James Aloysius Hickey.

I close with an insightful observation by Sister Mary Rose McGeady, head of Covenant House.

> The founder of my religious order, St. Vincent de Paul, taught us that before we can teach the poor about God we must first take care of their bodily needs. At Covenant House, we can't tell a kid God loves her if she's dirty, cold, hungry, and sick.
>
> Words like love don't work on our kids. We are challenged as Christians to *show* our kids we love them, not tell them.[7]

Can we, Christ's little children ourselves, show our Catholic people that we love our battered little children, that we love these crucified images of the Christ child?

Sacred Heart Retreat and Renewal Center
Youngstown, Ohio
January 3, 1994

SEVEN LAST WORDS OF JESUS

3

FATHER, FORGIVE THEM
The First Word

• Luke 23:34

Every so often, as I read Scripture, I find myself surprised, at times shocked. The latest shock? The first words of Jesus from his final cross: "Father, forgive them, for they do not know what they are doing" (Lk 23:34a). Why shocked? I had picked up a first-rate Catholic translation of Luke's Gospel. To my surprise, those words were not part of the translation. Why not? The translator told us why. Those words do not appear in very early manuscripts of Luke, important manuscripts, manuscripts from different geographical areas; they are absent from some ancient translations. And so the question arises: Did these words really form part of Luke's own text?[1]

How did I recover from the shock? When I realized, deep down, that it doesn't really matter whether Jesus *spoke* those words from the cross. Surprised? Don't be. You see, apart from forgiveness Bethlehem and Calvary make no sense. The crib and the cross are themselves mute cries, unforgettable cries, for forgiveness—Bethlehem the beginning, Calvary the climax. To grasp this, we must mull over three remarkably real realities: sin, our Savior, ourselves.

I

Behind Calvary, hovering over the cross, is a terrifying three-letter word: sin. Most Americans prefer not to think about sin, gloss over it. Sin, we are told, is a Catholic guilt trip. Sin is a weapon the circuit riders used, televangelists still use, to literally "scare the hell" out of us and our money with it. Sin doesn't make sense in a sophisticated culture.

The reality is dreadfully different. Sin is why God's unique Son borrowed our flesh and nailed it to a cross. Sin, you see, makes for separation. On four levels. First, sin severs us from our God. To sin seriously is not simply to manipulate a Savings & Loan, not simply to sleep with another person's spouse. To sin is to break a bond, to destroy a relationship, to withdraw *myself* from God and God's love. Recall Eden's garden and the very first temptation: If you eat the fruit forbidden, "you will be like God" (Gen 3:5). Recall the first man saying no to the God who had shaped him from love, had shaped him for love.

Second, sin severs us within our very selves. In sin I am inwardly divided, I am not the one person God shaped me to be. Recall the schizophrenia St. Paul deplored: "I do not understand my own actions; for I do not do what I want, I do the very thing I hate" (Rom 7:15). Made to God's image, I cease to image God.

Third, sin severs us from one another. How? Because sin destroys community, weakens the family God had in mind when creating. Recall murderer Cain responding to God's question, "Where is your brother Abel?" "I don't know. Am I my brother's keeper?" (Gen 4:9). Recall the six million of our Jewish sisters and brothers massacred by one man's hate. Recall the hatreds that sever rich and poor, black and white, man and woman.

Fourth, sin severs us from the earth. Recall how we rape the earth that nourishes us, ravage it with our pollution and pesticides, our waste and our indifference. And notice how the things we have taken for granted are now refusing to be our slaves any longer, how earth and sea and sky are taking their revenge on us, how the monster we have fashioned threatens to strangle us.

II

The solution to sin? An incredibly imaginative God. A God who willed to save us from sin and from ourselves. How? Not by sending an angel with a telegram of forgiveness. The evangelist John says it all: "God so loved the world that God gave God's only Son, so that everyone who believes in him may not perish but may have eternal life" (Jn 3:16). "Gave" is such an inadequate monosyllable. God's Son took our flesh. He was born of a mother's flesh as we are born. He grew in knowledge and wisdom as we grow, from a mother and father and teachers of the law. For three years he was as homeless as the lepers he healed. He found out what it feels like to grow hungry and tired, to have his relatives think him mad and his townsfolk try to toss him over a cliff. He felt thorns in his brow and lashes on his back, experienced what Godforsakenness feels like, died as we die, not with experience of resurrection but with faith in his Father, with hope of life without end.

One word sums up Jesus' living and dying: compassion. In Jesus God's compassion took flesh. He is, in the profound expression of Scripture, "God with us." In him God enters history, our history, as a suffering God, a God who wore our weakness, felt our fright, swallowed our bitter cup of rejection and loneliness. He is compassion incarnate, God's compassion in weak human flesh. Everything he did from Bethlehem to Calvary welled up from the bowels of his compassion. Not a cold concept; compassion is love pervading the whole person.

And Calvary? Calvary is the climax of compassion. Yes indeed, Calvary is itself God's cry of forgiveness. But not some vague word of pardon, "I forgive you." Calvary's forgiveness is a massive, marvelous work of reconciliation. Calvary's forgiveness makes possible the unity, the oneness, on four levels that existed in Eden and sin destroyed. (1) Once again, as in Eden, I can be one with my God in intimate love, share the life of Father, Son, and Holy Spirit alive within me. (2) With Christ's grace I can be one whole person, at peace within myself despite my woeful weaknesses, no longer torn inside by Satan, by sin, by self. (3) With the dynamism of the Holy Spirit, I have the power to root out the petty dislikes and the inhuman hatreds that dis-member the human family, the capacity to love my sisters and brothers as Christ loved and loves me. (4) Once again, as in Eden, I can reverence the earth on which I dance so lightly, become the steward of God's creation and not its despot, care for the things of God of which God said on the sixth day of creation, "It is very good" (Gen 1:31).

III

Finally, what of us? Forgiveness raises problems in three ways. First, I can despair of God's forgiveness. In my sinfulness I can repeat the despairing cry of Cain to the Lord, "My punishment is greater than I can bear" (Gen 4:13). My sins are too monstrous to be forgiven. No. If such is your shame, kneel before the Christ of Calvary. See those wounds not as God's anger at sinful humankind, "Look what you've done to me!" See those wounds as God's compassion, "Look how utterly I love you!" The only reality more powerful than sin is love—God's love and yours.

A second problem: I can refuse to forgive myself. Strange creatures that we are, we can beat on ourselves, scourge our spirits, without mercy. Sorrow is indeed demanded when my sin has said to God "I will not obey," said to a sister or brother "I hate you." But sorrow is not an end in itself; sorrow is a fresh beginning. Genuine sorrow says to a crucified Christ, "If you could die for love of me, I can at least live for love of you."

A third problem: the prayer our Lord left us, the petition in the Our Father, "Forgive us our sins as we forgive those who sin against us." As we forgive. Every so often I must ask myself: Do I really mean that? To the extent that I forgive others, to that extent, dear Lord, I want you to forgive me? I am not about to solve complex issues of forgiveness. Should Palestinians forgive the Brooklyn Jew who murdered 29 of their brothers and sisters in a Hebron mosque? Should an American Jew forgive the Nazis who gassed his parents a half century ago? These are complex questions not solved in a homily. Rather than exhort you from a pinnacle of ignorance—ignorance of you and your real problems—let me close with a true story that stems from the Middle East not long ago.

In the Hashemite Kingdom of Jordan, in a tiny town named Mafraq, two Bedouin youths got into a fight, fell to the ground in their fury. One lad pulled out a knife, plunged it fatally into the other's flesh. In fear he fled for days across the desert, fled the slain boy's vengeful relatives, fled to find a Bedouin sanctuary, a "tent of refuge" designed by law for those who kill unintentionally or in the heat of anger. At last he reached what might be a refuge—the black-tented encampment of a nomad tribe. He flung himself at the feet of its leader, an aged sheik, begged him: "I have killed in the heat of anger; I implore your protection; I seek the refuge of your tent."

"If God wills," the old man responded, "I grant it to you, as long as you remain with us."

A few days later the avenging relatives tracked the fugitive to the refuge. They asked the sheik: "Have you seen this man? Is he here? For we will have him."

"He is here, but you will not have him."

"He has killed, and we the blood relatives of the slain will stone him by law."

"You will not."

"We demand him!"

"No. The boy has my protection. I have given my word, my promise of refuge."

"But you do not understand. He has killed your grandson!"

The ancient sheik was silent. No one dared to speak. Then, in visible pain, with tears searing his face, the old man stood up and spoke ever so slowly: "My only grandson—he is dead?"

"Yes, your only grandson is dead."

"Then," said the sheik, "then this boy will be my son. He is forgiven, and he will live with us as my own. Go now; it is finished."[2]

4
TODAY YOU WILL BE WITH ME IN PARADISE
The Second Word

• Luke 23:43

Three grown men—all crucified together as criminals. What thoughts are running through their heads as life seeps out of their bodies? Two of them—Jews or unbelievers, we know not; we know only that they were bandits, robbers, highwaymen. Both of these focus on the man in the middle. One of them is intent only on a last-minute, Houdini-type escape. He takes his cue from the mocking mob, provokes the man in the middle: "Aren't you the Messiah? [Then] save yourself and us!" The other bandit harbors no thought of escape; he moves in a different direction. He admits his guilt, rebukes his fellow felon: "On the edge of death, don't you even fear God? We have been condemned justly, but this man has done nothing wrong." Then, under a stunning gift of grace, he acknowledges the kingly status of the convict in the middle: "Remember me when you come into your kingdom." Jesus' reply is equally stunning: "Believe me, today you will be with me in paradise" (Lk 23:39-43).

Why is this episode so important to Luke's account of the Passion? To answer that, let's focus on three questions. (1) What is the significance of the "good thief"? (2) What is the significance of the "bad thief"? (3) What might these two convicts be saying of significance to you and me?

I

First, the good thief. Why is he so significant that Luke includes the episode in his Gospel? Because here is the high point in Luke's story of Calvary. Here you have in miniature the story of salvation, all in five swift verses. The episode summarizes with startling vividness what the Son of God took our flesh to effect. It tells us what Calvary did for all of us by narrating what Calvary did for one of us. It illustrates what Jesus said when the Pharisees and scribes complained about him to his disciples, "Why does he eat with toll collectors and sinners?" Jesus told them why: "The healthy have no need of a physician, but the sick do. I have not come to call the upright to repentance, but sinners" (Mk 2:16-17; Lk 5:30-32).

On Calvary one specific sinner, a bandit, admits he is a sinner, is guilty of thievery and perhaps much else. He recognizes that he and his comrade are suffering "justly, for we are only getting what we deserve for our deeds" (Lk 23:41). And he turns to Jesus, not really knowing who Jesus is. He doesn't call him "Lord"; he calls him "Jesus." But somehow, through all the blood and sweat and tears, the kingly quality of Jesus has come through to him. He is sorry for his sins; he asks this stranger, this just man, this "king" to remember him. He pleads that Jesus remember him in a future he cannot even imagine. He "asks for a share in the mercy that only a king can dispense."[1]

And Jesus? As St. Ambrose of Milan put it 15 centuries ago, "More abundant is the favor shown than the request made."[2] As so often, Jesus responds with a generosity that exceeds the request: "Today you will be with me." Don't spend much time on the word "today." It does not mean the calendar day of the crucifixion, Jesus and the good thief meeting in heaven the first Good Friday. It means the day of salvation inaugurated by the death of Jesus.[3] It means he will be with Jesus always. Here is salvation at its simplest and most stunning: the repentant sinner with Jesus days without end.

II

Second question: What is the significance of the bad thief? Picture the scene once again. Two sinners are pinned to crosses. Crosses very much like Jesus' own. Each is crucified *next to* Jesus. But only one is crucified *with* Jesus. He is the one who confessed his crimes, expressed his sorrow, professed his desire to be with Jesus in his kingdom, even sympathized with the innocent man crucified so close to him. The other? All he could think of was how to escape, how this fellow who was supposed to be the Messiah might use his magic to get all three off their crosses. "Save yourself and us!" (Lk 23:39). How ironic! "*Save* us."

Briefly, it is the dark side of salvation's story. The side where "save" has only one meaning: Get me off my cross! It is the oft-repeated mocking cry on Calvary. The cry of the people's leaders: "If you're the Messiah, if you're God's chosen one, save yourself." The cry of the soldiers: "If you're the King of the Jews, save yourself!" (vv. 35-37). This cry, I suspect, may well have torn the heart of Jesus more than any other. The cross was to be the whole world's way to salvation. And the world would never cease crying with the chief priests and scribes, "Come down from the cross now, so that we may see and believe" (Mk 15:32). Come down.

He could have, of course. But at what cost to us? Which compels my third question: What might these two convicts be saying to you and me?

III

Back in 1982 Graham Greene published a delightful novel titled *Monsignor Quixote*. On a journey with a remarkable Communist mayor, the Spanish priest has a "terrible dream" that stays with him "like a cheap tune in the head."

> He had dreamt that Christ had been saved from the Cross by the legion of angels to which on an earlier occasion the Devil had told Him that He could appeal. So there was no final agony, no heavy stone which had to be rolled away, no discovery of an empty tomb. Father Quixote stood there watching on Golgotha as Christ stepped down from the Cross triumphant and acclaimed. The Roman soldiers, even the Centurion, knelt in His honor, and the people of Jerusalem poured up the hill to worship Him. The disciples clustered happily around. His mother smiled through her tears of joy. There was no ambiguity, no room for doubt and no room for faith at all. The whole world knew with certainty that Christ was the Son of God.
>
> It was only a dream, of course it was only a dream, but nonetheless Father Quixote had felt on waking the chill of despair felt by a man who realizes suddenly that he has taken up a profession which is of use to no one, who must continue to live in a kind of Saharan desert without doubt or faith, where everyone is certain that the same belief is true. He had found himself whispering, "God save me from such a belief."[4]

Yes, Jesus could have come down from the cross. When Father, Son, and Holy Spirit had their summit session in secret on how best to save the world, the Trinity could have opted for all sorts of triumphant scenarios, including Father Quixote's dream. Why this one, with a God/man bleeding out his life on a criminal's cross, refusing to come down? The best answer we humans can concoct was phrased by Jesus himself: "God so loved the world..." (Jn 3:16). Or more personally in the exultant cry of St. Paul, "The Son of God loved me and gave himself for me" (Gal 2:20). And it may well be true that the surest way of attracting my love is not by a triumphant display of divine power but through a God-man actually experiencing what it means to be human, to laugh and cry, to be born and die.

So then, thanks be to God for the two criminals justly crucified on Calvary. The bad thief tells me it is not enough for me to be nailed *next to* Christ; the good thief tells me I must be crucified *with* Christ. It is then that I can say sincerely with St. Paul, "I am now rejoicing in my sufferings for your sake, and in my flesh I am completing what is lacking in Christ's afflictions for the sake of his body, the Church" (Col 1:24).

Quite some years ago an imaginative preacher proclaimed that on his cross the good thief pulled off his most thrilling theft: He stole heaven. A precious thought, but not quite true. No one steals heaven. I reach paradise, I reach God, by God's gracious giving. And I reach it by linking my cross with Christ's. His challenge is unmistakable: If I want to be his disciple, if I want to follow him, I must "take up [my] cross every day" (Lk 9:23).

The cross is there, often almost unbearable. Even Jesus discovered this. But I do not make the cross bearable by coming down from it. It becomes bearable when I am crucified *with* Christ. The good thief discovered that.

5
WOMAN, LOOK! YOUR SON....
LOOK! YOUR MOTHER
The Third Word

• John 19:26-27

In the Greek text, nine remarkable words; puzzling words. Too complex for a short homily, too rich for a single meditation. So, let me suggest a way of seeing this Gospel scene that has three distinct advantages. It has the backing of some fine biblical scholars; it fits in beautifully with the symbolism we find in the evangelist John; and it makes for solid, yet thrilling devotion to our Lady.

I

You can, if you wish, see in this scene only what is obvious. With the thoughtful compassion that was characteristic of his whole ministry, the dying Jesus makes sure that his mother will be cared for after his death. This is the way some of the early Christian theologians and preachers understood Jesus' words; and an age-old tradition maintains that after Jesus' death John did take Mary to Ephesus in Asia Minor, to live in his home.

Think of it this way, and theologians like myself will not complicate your prayer life. You can rest happy that one of Jesus' last thoughts was of his mother, a mother who had lost her husband and now was losing her only son. Even if he "ran away" from Mary and Joseph in Jerusalem at the age of 12, Jesus was a good son, a devoted son. Remember Luke's words, "He was obedient to them" (Lk 2:51). He loved his mother, cared deeply for her, was concerned in his last agony how to provide for her livelihood in a culture where a widow could not inherit from her husband, was an obvious victim for unscrupulous creditors, had no defender at law, was at the mercy of dishonest judges.[1]

II

Yes, Jesus was thinking of his mother. But there is more here than meets the eye. You see, John's Gospel is brimful of symbols. I mean external signs that work mysteriously on the human consciousness so as to suggest more than they can clearly describe or define, are pregnant with a depth of meaning evoked rather than explicitly stated.[2] Symbols are not strange, "off-the-wall" stuff that eggheads dream up on college campuses. Symbols make up much of human living. Think of the Stars and Stripes or the Confederate flag; think of stretch limos or MTV; think of Madonna or Martin Luther King Jr.; think of the Lamb of God; think of the Christian cross.

And now turn back to John. That John had something in mind more profound than Jesus' filial care for his mother is suggested several times. You have that exclamation "Look!"[3] In John it is a formula he uses several times when he wants to reveal the mystery of a person's mission. "Look!", John the Baptist exclaims to two of his disciples as they watch Jesus walk by. "Look! The Lamb of God" (Jn 1:29).[4] Now here, with John himself standing next to Mary beneath the cross. "Look!", Jesus murmurs to his mother. "Your son." Then to John: "Look! Your mother" (Jn 19:26-27). With that scene in mind, recall the marriage feast at Cana. Only at Cana and on Calvary does John speak of Jesus' mother. In both scenes Jesus addresses his mother as "Woman"—not an impolite term at all. Not much different from "Lady Mother." You remember how at the wedding Jesus at first said no to Mary's request for more wine: "My hour has not yet come" (Jn 2:4). On Calvary Jesus' "hour" has come, and Mary receives her role in God's plan for our salvation. In fact, John suggests a deeper meaning when he goes on to say, "After this, [Jesus was] aware that all was now finished" (Jn 19:28)—all that the Father had given him to do.[5]

But what precisely is the striking symbolism here? At this climactic hour in the redemption of our world, through the death of God's unique Son, men and women are to be re-created, created anew, as God's children. And Jesus tells us that John and Mary, his "beloved disciple" and his mother, are symbols. John symbolizes, represents, stands for the Christian, for each and every sister and brother of Christ. And Mary symbolizes, represents, stands for the Church, which, like Lady Zion in the Hebrew Testament, after her birth pangs brings forth a new people in joy. Very simply, Mary beneath the cross becomes a symbol of the Church—the Church that must bring forth children modeled after Jesus. And Mary with John is a symbol of "the relationship that must bind the children to their mother."[6]

III

And all this brings us to...ourselves. What of us? The scene on Calvary brings a Catholic face to face with two realities inseparable from Catholicism: our Lady and our Church. Several decades ago we almost "lost" our Lady. All too many Catholics felt we were paying too much attention to her, were paying her worship instead of veneration, were contrasting the "mother of mercy" with the just judge Jesus. They were trying to put Mary "in her place." And the result was...no place. The rosary disappeared, novenas, statues, vigil lights...Mary.

No, dear friends. We have come to see with extraordinary clarity how irreplaceable our Lady is. She is the mother of God's only Son—not only was, but is, right now and forever. She is the perfect disciple, the prime example of discipleship; for Mary, more perfectly than any other sheerly human person, heard the word of God and did it, said yes to God in Nazareth and has never stopped saying yes. And she reveals what insightful theologians call "the female face of God"; for she reveals in her own person aspects of God we tend to overlook: "[a]ll that is creative and generative of life, all that nourishes and nurtures, all that is benign, cherishes, and sustains, all that is full of solicitude and sympathy.... All mothering on earth has its source" in our mothering God.[7] Mary shows us all that, shows us what Pope John Paul I preached one Sunday in his short pontificate: God is not only father but "even more so mother," who wants only to love us, even and especially when we are bad.[8]

And this afternoon, beneath the cross, we see our Lady as symbol of the Church. She represents, she stands for, the Church, the sorrowful/joyful mother who under God brought me to new life in baptism, enlightens my mind with God's Word, feeds my soul at the Lord's Supper, cradles my dying flesh like another *Pietà*.

A paradox indeed, because ever so many baptized Catholics have found the living Church a paradox, perhaps even a contradiction. All too many have left her; for they have been ignored or insulted, misunderstood or misrepresented, dreadfully hurt, perhaps mortally wounded, by their Church, have fled to communities of Christian compassion. For all such, for all of us, let me close with a paragraph from the experience of a profound French theologian, Henri de Lubac. He had suffered much from the powerful in the Church, but I remember best hearing him declare of the Church to an international convention at Notre Dame:

> I am told that she is holy, yet I see her full of sinners. I am told that
> her mission is to tear [us] away from [our] earthy cares,...yet I see

her constantly preoccupied with the things of the earth and of time, as if she wished us to live here forever. I am assured that she is universal, as open as divine intelligence and charity, and yet I notice very often that her members...huddle together timidly in closed groups—as human beings do everywhere.... Nonetheless in this community I find my support, my strength, my joy. The Church, she is my mother.[9]

My support, my strength, my joy,...my mother. My Church. All this on the face of a sorrowing woman. "Look! Your mother."

6
WHY HAVE YOU FORSAKEN ME?
The Fourth Word

- Matthew 27:46
- Mark 15:34

For me, perhaps the most crucifying feeling in all the world would be to feel I am absolutely alone. To feel that nobody cares, no one loves me, it doesn't matter to anyone whether I live or die. When even the God in whom I have put my trust has withdrawn from me, doesn't seem to be there, perhaps doesn't care.

I

Do we actually discover such a moment as we stand beneath the cross? At about three o'clock on a dark Friday, a crucified Jew named Jesus cries out "with a loud voice, 'My God, my God, why have you forsaken me?'" (Mt 27:46; Mk 15:34). It boggles my mind. The Jesus of whom the Father declared, "This is the Son I love; with him I am well pleased" (Mt 17:5); the Jesus who could say, "The One who sent me... has not left me alone" (Jn 8:29); the Jesus who is at the point of realizing all that he took flesh to do, of consummating history's most remarkable act of love, of saving humankind from sin and self and Satan; the Jesus who is surrounded by mocking enemies, has seen his dearest friends scatter in fear, has just given his mother to the disciple he loves most—can he really be experiencing in all its dread reality the absence of *God*, the absence of his Father?

In my younger years I reacted with a loud and clear no. Not Jesus; not God's own Son in flesh. There was good reason not to take Jesus' cry of abandonment in its obvious sense. After all, Scripture scholars reminded us that Jesus was simply reciting Psalm 22, the cry of a just man in profound desolation:

> My God, my God, why have you forsaken me?
>> Why are you so far from helping me,
>> from the words of my groaning?
> O my God, I cry by day, but you do not answer;
>> and by night, but find no rest.
>
> (Ps 22:1-2)

No, I said. At its most extreme, this is the kind of exaggeration you express when life is at its lowest, when the bottom has fallen out of all you hold dear. After all, Jesus does say "*My* God, *my* God." In such a cry how can God seem to be totally absent?

II

In the gathering twilight of my existence I am no longer so sure. Jesus is not playacting; his passion is not make-believe. Remember why Jesus took our flesh, was born as we are born. God could have worked our salvation in so many different ways. But God decided to save us through a flesh like ours, through a God-*man*. God's Son became one of us because he wanted to experience what we experience as we experience it. Recall the New Testament Letter to the Hebrews: "We do not have a high priest who is unable to sympathize with our weaknesses, but one who in every respect has been tested as we are, yet without sin" (Heb 4:15). The Jesus who took to himself not only our flesh but all that makes us human short of sin took to himself our loneliness. The loneliness of every mother for the child of her womb, be he treacherous like Judas, repentant as Peter, warm as John. The loneliness of the friendless, the outcast, the refugee, the aged. The loneliness of every human crucified between heaven and earth, unable to see God for the clouds, dear ones through tears.

Not despair, not hopelessness. Jesus did indeed experience feelings of loneliness, of abandonment, of Godforsakenness we can scarcely begin to imagine. But he never stopped trusting. It is indeed a cry of desolation: God has given him over to his enemies. And for all his decision to die for us, his flesh rebelled against it. Remember his agonizing prayer in Gethsemane: "Father, if you are willing, remove this cup from me" (Lk 22:42). Dear God, don't let me die! Yet, like the just man in Psalm 22, he continues to say "*My* God, *my* God." And it is the whole of Psalm 22, not only the first line, that lingers in his cry of abandonment:

> In you our ancestors trusted;
>> they trusted, and you delivered them.

> To you they cried, and were saved;
>   in you they trusted, and were not put to shame.
>   (Ps 22:4-5)

III

And what of us? Several weeks ago I spoke individually with two young women. Each had experienced crushing loss in a death. One had lost her father, kept asking, "Where is he now?", could only pray one prayer, "God, please exist!" The other had lost her baby after about 14 weeks of pregnancy, and with it lost the sense, the feeling, of God's all-pervading presence, now finds a huge hole in her life where prayer used to be. In effect, each is asking, "My God, my God, why have you forsaken me?"

Good friends, loneliness, a sense of forsakenness, seems to go hand in hand with human living. It is a sorrow increasingly ours as the years hasten by, as God strips from us, one by one, as God stripped Jesus, the attachments that are the bittersweet of life on earth: the people we love, the things we cherish, yes life itself. And, you know, some of the most remarkable saints in our history experienced what is called "the dark night of the soul," could not find God anywhere, dried up in prayer, questioned whether God even cared.

It happens. Is there any answer to feeling forsaken, even by God? I have no automatic push button, infallible for any and every Christian. I suggest a twin approach. First, I must link my feeling of Godforsaken-ness to Jesus' own sense of abandonment by his Father. Why? Because Jesus' experience of frightful aloneness on the cross, like his hunger in the desert, like his sweat of blood in the garden, was not some isolated incident, unconnected with anything else; it was part and parcel of his redemptive role. I mean, it played its part in bringing God's grace, God's love, to sinful humankind, to you and me. Linked to our Lord, offered to our Lord, my feeling of being forsaken, abandoned, can course through this Body of Christ that is the Church, can be used by God to ease the crucifixion of a sister or brother ever so close to despair.

Second, like the just person in Psalm 22, I too can murmur from the depths of dereliction, "*My* God." For, as someone phrased it with rare felicity, God does not forsake us unless we first forsake God. And even then the words of the Lord to Israel in exile ring true:

> Can a woman forget her nursing child,
>   or show no compassion for the child of her womb?
> Even these may forget,
>   yet I will not forget you.

> See, I have inscribed you on the palms of my hands.
> (Isa 49:15)

No matter what, God is there, God is here. Believe it, especially when you cannot sense it, cannot feel it. Believe it or not, God cares—infinitely more than you and I do.

Dear forsaken Savior: There is a fresh urgency among many today that you have somehow forsaken your Church. In the agonies that torment us as individuals and as an institution, in the infidelities and injustices that foul our Christian nest, your face is so hard to find. Grace us this sacred day to sense your ceaseless presence: in our coming together, in the Word we hear proclaimed, in the Bread we share, in your image on the faces of the unfortunate, those who cry from empty stomachs or empty hearts, "My God, my God, why have you forsaken me?"

7
I AM THIRSTY
The Fifth Word

• John 19:28

A single Greek word in John's Gospel: *dipso*. "I am thirsty" (Jn 19:28). Simple on the face of it, but there's more than meets the eye, a depth of meaning that no Greek dictionary by itself could capture.

I

On the face of it, two realities seem clear enough. First, Jesus was physically thirsty; his lips, his mouth, his throat were terribly dry. How could they fail to be? In prison overnight, back lashed with whips, head crowned with thorns, a cross on his back from jail to Golgotha, his back on a cross for three hours—how he must have yearned for the water he had asked of the Samaritan woman, for that cup of cold water he told us to give to others in his name! Perhaps he remembered his parable of the rich man and Lazarus, the prayer of the rich man in hell: "Father Abraham, have mercy on me, and send Lazarus to dip the tip of his finger in water and cool my tongue, for I am in agony in these flames" (Lk 16:24). Yes, Jesus wanted water.[1]

Second fact: As John tells us, Jesus said he was thirsty "to bring the Scripture to its complete fulfilment." What Scripture? Perhaps Psalm 69:21: "For my food they gave me something bitter; for my thirst, sour wine." Possibly Psalm 22:15: "My mouth is dried up like a potsherd, and my tongue sticks to my jaws."

Make no mistake. Even bringing Scripture to its fulfilment did not wet the lips of Jesus. He suffered the thirst of the damned; he was as thirsty as the wealthy man in hell.

34

II

Simple explanations these; they make good sense, stay close to the facts. But once again let me suggest something even more enriching for our understanding of Calvary. It has to do with the evangelist John and his symbolism. I mean his frequent use of words and phrases that suggest more than they can explicitly say. How can we connect Jesus' "I am thirsty" with John's own symbolism?

Start with a Gospel incident surely familiar to you. You remember how Peter, to protect Jesus, drew his sword and cut off the right ear of Malchus, the high priest's slave. What did Jesus say to Peter? "Put your sword back into its sheath. Am I not to drink the cup that the Father has given me?" (Jn 18:11). What cup? Suffering and dying. Recall Jesus kneeling in Gethsemane, sweating blood because his flesh shrank from suffering, from dying, yet praying: "Father, if you are willing, remove this cup from me; yet, not my will but yours be done" (Lk 22:42). On the cross the sheer physical thirst, the kind of thirst you feel after a day without water in the desert, was intense indeed; but the physical thirst was not uppermost in Jesus' mind. Above all else, Jesus thirsted to drink the cup of suffering and dying, drink it to its last drop. Why? Because only when he had tasted the bitter wine of death would his Father's will be fulfilled.[2]

What, then, was Jesus' deepest yearning, far more than for water or wine? Very simply, he wanted to complete what he had been born to do. More than anything else in life, he wanted to die. For us. Out of pure love.

III

And what of us? This afternoon we are not spectators on Calvary, even sympathetic spectators, keeping a death watch outside Jerusalem, sadly watching a good man die. Calvary is today; the cup is our cup. The cup is our suffering, our dying. Not a morbid concentration on our last breath, but thirst as our share in the redemption wrought by Jesus. St. Paul put it pungently for all of us to the Christians of Colossae in Asia Minor: "I am now rejoicing in my sufferings for your sake, and in my flesh I am completing what is lacking in Christ's sufferings for the sake of his body, that is, the Church" (Col 1:24). It is our task as Christians, as followers of Christ, to carry on his work of redemption, to bring his life to our acre of God's world.

This is not masochism, "Pile it on, Lord!" In itself, suffering is neither good nor bad. The critical question is, why? What gives suffering meaning? What transmutes sheer suffering into sacrifice? On Calvary it was love, "God so loved the world" (Jn 3:16). "As the Father has loved me, so I have loved you" (Jn 14:9). But why life through death? Jesus put it strongly: "Unless the grain of wheat falls into the earth and dies, it remains alone [just a single grain]; but if it dies, it bears much fruit" (Jn 12:24). It is the paschal mystery: no Easter without its Good Friday.

The dying is not simply our last breath; the dying is the cross every day, total self-giving to God for others. Such has been the Christian experience since Calvary, the "I thirst" of Christ's community. In our own time, Dorothy Day giving life and love to New York's downtrodden by sharing their squalor, living literally with their rats and their diseases. Black Franciscan Thea Bowman changing lives by wheeling her cancer across the country, praying one ceaseless prayer, "Lord, let me live until I die," let me "live, love, and serve fully until death comes."[3] Martin Luther King Jr. exposing heart and brain to gunshots so that all God's children might be "free at last." Lutheran Dietrich Bonhoeffer walking to Nazi gallows without fear, ceaselessly preaching that our likeness to God is a question of relationships: To be free is to be for the other. Mother Teresa cradling Calcutta's rejects, Beirut's orphans, D.C.'s HIV-positives, so that all might at least die with dignity. Polish Franciscan Maximilian Kolbe taking the place of a married man destined for Nazi death, so that the man might be alive for his family.

The point is, all of these were athirst out of love. Love not for a God in outer space, but for a Christ crucified outside Jerusalem. Love not for an abstract humanity, but for each human image of God. So thirsty that it hurt, physically hurt, to hear the cries of the poor, to gaze upon hunger-stretched stomachs, to touch the fevered or ice-cold flesh of the homeless, to smell the stench of another's dying.

My thirsty Jesus: My own lips, I discover, do get bitterly dry. But usually it is because I am afraid...for myself. A straitjacket, a predicament, from which there is no escaping. Rarely am I parched because each year in our land of the free 1.6 million helpless humans are violently prevented from being born; because one of every five American children grows up hungry; because a million youngsters sleep on our streets each night, many angel-dusted and prostituted; because children in D.C. are so exposed to violence that they are preparing their own funerals; because the elderly in my area rummage in garbage cans for the food I cast away so lightly; because millions of refugees are watering the world's ways with their tears. So then, dear Jesus, make my tongue cleave to my jaws. Make me thirst for the kind of love that brings life to the lifeless. In a word, dear Lord, awaken your Spirit within me, to inflame my heart, so that I may touch others with the flame of your love. Let my profound prayer each day begin..."I am thirsty."

8
IT IS FINISHED
The Sixth Word

• John 19:30

It is close to three o'clock. The sun has shrouded its face for shame, and a blackness as of hell is come to mourn over Calvary. For the Lord through whom "all things came into being" (Jn 1:3) hangs helplessly poised between the heaven and earth of his creating hand. And from his parched lips issues a quiet declaration: "It is finished" (Jn 19:30).

I

What is finished? Is this simply a sigh of gratitude, "It's all over at last—no more pain, no more blood"? No; not at all. Then what is finished? Why, all that God's Son took flesh to do. Eden is swallowed up in Calvary, Adam in Christ, Eve in Mary, sin in satisfaction. As St. Paul would put it to the Christians of Rome: Just as by the disobedience of one man, the first man, Adam, the mass of humanity was estranged from God, so by the obedience of one man, Jesus Christ, the mass of humanity would be made upright, the sinner become just, the guilty stand before God acquitted, innocent (cf. Rom 5:19).[1] It is the realization of Jesus' promise, "And I, when I am lifted up from the earth, will draw all men and women to myself" (Jn 12:32). "Now," Jesus had promised, "now will the Prince of this world [Satan] be driven out" (v. 31). His mission from the Father is now completed.

Where is Jesus' work finished, his mission completed? Here? On a cross? With nails piercing his hands and feet? With Roman soldiers gambling for his garments? With a mocking mob shaking fists in his face, challenging him to save himself? With a robber at his right hand and a robber at his left? Forsaken by most of his friends and seemingly

by his Father? Yes, if ever proof were needed that God's ways are not
our ways, the proof beams like a beacon from the blackness of Calvary.
The most incredible love in the world's history is consummated in the
most horrible crime.

Why is Jesus' work finished here? Why, as Judas might put it, why
this waste? Why could not God's Son have thought of a cheaper
redemption than Calvary? Very simply, he could have. He could have
redeemed us in Bethlehem, just by being born. In Nazareth, with a
single act of obedience to Joseph. In the desert, with one pang of
hunger. In Gethsemane, with one drop of bloody sweat. With a word,
"Your sins are forgiven you." Then why this waste?

II

A mystery indeed; for God's love escapes our earth-bound
intelligence. But perhaps the First Epistle of Peter casts some light:
"Christ suffered for you, leaving you an example, so that you should
follow in his steps" (1 Pet 2:21). We need not only God's forgiveness for
our sinfulness; we need Christ's example for our daily living. We need a
crucifix on our walls and in our hearts if we are to live as we were
originally shaped, like God, in God's image; if we are to link God's
forgiveness to the trials and agonies of human living; if we are not to
imitate fratricidal Cain and ask callously of God, "Am I my brother's
[and sister's] keeper?" (Gen 4:9); if we are not to be seduced by the
rugged individualism that tells us our ultimate responsibility is to
ourselves, because in the last analysis each of us is alone.

To love as Jesus loved, we had to see divine love in our flesh. We
had to see with our own eyes the kind of love that makes us divine. We
had to see God's own Son born as we are born, growing up as we grow,
hungering as we hunger, homeless and hated, friend of sinners and
outcasts, cradling little children and touching outcast lepers, caring for
all no matter what they looked like, revealing by his life what it means
to love God above all else and to love especially our less fortunate
sisters and brothers as if we were standing in their shoes. And God
clearly felt we could learn most powerfully how to love if we were to
join Jesus' mother beneath his cross and simply...look. The First Letter
of John says it all in a single sentence: "We know love by this, that
[Jesus] laid down his life for us—and we ought to lay down our lives for
one another" (1 Jn 3:16).

You see, in a genuine sense Jesus' work is *not* finished. Not
finished as long as a single woman or man remains on earth. Salvation
is not a push-button affair. Because of Calvary, salvation is indeed here

and now, in every age, at every moment. For all the hatred and violence that surround us, the world is different since Calvary. Grace, God's favor and love, is the air we breathe. Still, grace has to be touched to each man or woman born into the world. Has to be touched to you and me, and through you and me to the men and women whose paths we are privileged to cross. Privileged indeed; for this is our share in the redeeming love that climaxed on Calvary.

III

What then? A realization and a resolution. The realization? At the pierced feet of Jesus, I need never fear that I walk alone, that Jesus doesn't really understand what I have to go through, that it's easy enough for him to say, "Take up your cross." No, each cross of mine is Jesus' cross; he carried it on Calvary; he carries it now with me.

The resolution? If I am not called to die for my sisters and brothers, I can at least live for them. I believe it was a Sufi mystic who asked God why He didn't do something for the unfortunates of the world. God is reported to have replied, "I did. I made you." I *must* live for the crucified images of Christ. For the work Jesus came to do can only be finished through you and me. In this task we are not alone. We are members of a body St. Paul called "the body of Christ" (1 Cor 12:27). In this body no one, pope included, can say to any other, "I have no need of you" (v. 21). Paul told us bluntly, "If one member suffers, all suffer together with it" (v. 26). I recommend to you enthusiastically an image preached by Presbyterian Frederick Buechner. He compared humanity to an enormous spider web.

> If you touch it anywhere, you set the whole thing trembling.... As we move around this world and as we act with kindness, perhaps, or with indifference, or with hostility, toward the people we meet, we too are setting the great spider web a-tremble. The life that I touch for good or ill will touch another life, and that in turn another, until who knows where the trembling stops or in what far place and time my touch will be felt. Our lives are linked. No man [no woman] is an island....[2]

Deepen that thought. Recall that it is God who gives the increase. The Catholic belief in the "communion of saints" is a thrilling conviction: The Church on earth, the Church in heaven, the Church in purgatory, we are not alone, isolated. This is one enormous community linked together by the inexhaustible grace that flows from Christ and the cross. You and I can do nothing that is not felt, does not resonate, somewhere else in the body of Christ, perhaps throughout the body.

Living this conviction, good friends, you and I will be able on our own final calvary to murmur with Christ to the Father, "The work you gave me to do—it is finished."

9
INTO YOUR HANDS I ENTRUST MY SPIRIT
The Seventh Word

• Luke 23:46

I

For years I meditated on the final words[1] of Jesus with youthful simplicity. They seemed so natural, so obvious—just what a disciple of Jesus expects to hear from the lips of his Master. Here Jesus repeats a verse from one of the Hebrew Psalms (31:5), a psalm where the psalmist prays for deliverance from enemies and expresses his confidence in God:

> Incline your ear to me;
>> rescue me speedily.
> Be a rock of refuge for me,
>> a strong fortress to save me.
> You are indeed my rock and my fortress;
>> for your name's sake lead me and guide me,
> take me out of the net that is hidden for me,
>> for you are my refuge.
> Into your hand I entrust my spirit;
>> you have redeemed me, O Lord, faithful God.
>>> (Ps 31:2-5)

In the later rabbinical tradition that lovely verse, "Into your hand I entrust my spirit," was used as part of an evening prayer a disciple should utter before going to sleep.[2] I murmur it myself as the Night Prayer of my breviary draws to a close. How touching it was for Jesus to surrender himself once and for all into the hands of the Father he loved above all else!

II

Only within recent years have I looked more deeply into that cry of ultimate surrender.[3] I have come to see how Scripture presents the life of Jesus not only as a life of love but as a remarkable wedding of *three* divine gifts: faith, hope, and love. It was in the unity of these three gifts that

> Jesus surrendered himself in his death unconditionally to the absolute mystery that he called his Father, into whose hands he committed his existence, when in the night of his death and God-forsakenness he was deprived of everything [we regard as] human existence.... Everything fell away from him, even the [secure feeling of God's intimate love], and in this trackless dark there prevailed silently only the mystery that...has no name and to which he...calmly surrendered himself as to eternal love and not to the hell of futility....[4]

The point is this. Even for Jesus, God's Son in human flesh, "death [was] the supreme and most radical act of faith."[5] Faith. Jesus believed, Jesus trusted, Jesus hoped. He was confident that he would rise again. But for your own consolation remember this: Jesus' own resurrection was not something of which he had personal experience; it was not something he could prove conclusively from sheer reason. For all that he was Son of God, this man died as we die: not with experience of resurrection, not with an unassailable logical argument. Jesus died with faith in his Father, with trust in a Father's love, with a living hope that he would live for ever.

It's so important to grasp this. For Jesus, death was not make-believe; death was a descent into darkness. Yes, he believed that at the end of the tunnel light would blaze. But he still had to face the dark, the unknown. And it was terrifying. Remember how in Gethsemane's garden the very nearness of death made him sweat blood—literally. It took an angel from heaven to give him strength. And in those last moments on the cross it took more than an angel; it took all the faith his Father had infused into him, all the hope he had harvested with his mother in Nazareth, all the trust he had shared with his disciples for three bittersweet years. It was with such faith, such hope, such trust that he could cry out with a loud voice, "Father, into your hands I entrust my spirit." I *entrust* my spirit. I surrender all I am to your love with confidence. And *so* "he bowed his head," *so* he "gave up his spirit" (Jn 19:30). It was not taken from him; he gave it, freely, to his Father.

III

And what of you and me? It's true, dying with Christ is not a single episode. For Christians, it should be a lifelong experience, letting go time and again of so much that is dear to us. Still, in each of our lives there will be a particularly critical moment, when God asks of us that we let go once and for all, let go of our earth-bound existence, all we call human living: home, dear ones, possessions, human touch, my very self. It is a movement into darkness, this severance of flesh and spirit, and it can be terrifying. And for good reasons. In the death of any person, something absolutely unique is lost. Not an "it," as when an animal dies. Years ago a Catholic philosopher put it powerfully when writing on the death of his wife: "When a human being dies, an 'I' is lost to the world and a 'thou' to the survivors."

For that hour there is no sheerly human panacea, no medicinal cure-all. Only one thing can transform this final hour from protest to acceptance, from an agonizing "Take this cup from me" to a peaceful "Into your hands." With St. Paul the Christian should be able to say, "To me, living is Christ and dying is gain" (Phil 1:21). But this conviction compels a new attitude. I dare not be "resigned" to death; that is insufficiently Christian; I am still looking on death as "the enemy." In contrast, insightful theologians insist that death should not be an experience I endure but an act I personally perform. Not euthanasia; simply an unconditional yes, an "I do." When Jesus cried, "Father, into your hands I entrust my spirit," he was affirming life. This is what I as a Christian must proclaim with my very last breath: I have life. Only with this attitude can death be an act I personally perform. *I die.*

It's not easy. I suggest it is feasible only if I have been following the Crucified, dying with him, through all or much of my living—what Karl Rahner called "all those brief moments of dying in installments."[6] If as a disciple of Christ I obey his injunction and take up my cross each day, the final cross may strike me as not simply inevitable but quite expectable—the final movement in a fascinating symphony.

Dear Lord: I think what frightens me is that monosyllable "death." It has such a ring of finality. Grace me to overshadow it with another monosyllable: life. Grace me to recall what you said to Lazarus' sister Martha when she confessed her belief that her brother "will rise again on the last day." You corrected her: "Those who believe in me, even though they die, will come to life; and everyone who is alive and believes in me will never die" (Jn 11:24-26).[7] Share with me the confidence you expressed with your last breath: your trust that "death" is as brief as the time it takes to murmur it. Let me trust your word that what you called "eternal life" (Jn 17:3), the life of the spirit, my life with you, does not end with the grave, in fact never ends. Let that be the faith in my heart as I murmur with my lips, "Father, into your hands I entrust my spirit."

St. James Cathedral
Seattle, Washington
April 1, 1994

ORDINARY
TIME

10

MY NAME IS LEGION, FOR WE ARE MANY
Fourth Week of the Year, Monday (B)

- 2 Samuel 15:13-14, 30; 16:5-13
- Mark 5:1-20

Today's Gospel exorcism raises at least four fascinating questions. (1) Was the poor fellow really possessed by a devil, by an "unclean spirit" (Mk 5:2)? (2) Is the name "legion" the spirit claimed for himself a subtle way of insulting the Roman legions occupying Palestine? (3) How do you justify the violent behavior of a peace-loving Jesus as he drives 2000 peaceful swine to destruction by drowning? (4) Aren't the Gerasenes justified in seeing Jesus as a public menace and consequently requesting him, "Don't go away mad, but please go away"?

But these are questions for scholars, for biblicists and ethicists. For believing Christians, two questions are far more pertinent: (1) What are the demons, the devils, that take possession of our American people today? (2) How can we drive them out?

I

First, can we identify some of the demons that possess our prevailing culture? I believe we can. Here I suggest three—these three because they should speak eloquently to men and women intent on preaching the just Word,[1] concerned to highlight those devilish, diabolical influences that keep Christians from living the just Word to the full, faithful to those relationships with God and people that stem from the covenant Christ struck with us in his blood.

The Superdemon? The devil that threatens the single family God had in mind when creating; threatens the world community shaped of sisters and brothers; threatens the Christ-Body within which no one can say to any other, "I have no need of you" (1 Cor 12:21); leads to the bone-chilling question Cain put to his God, "Am I my brother's keeper?" (Gen 4:9). I mean what Robert Bellah called a resurgence of late-19th-century rugged individualism, where the race is to the swift, the shrewd, the savage; where I had better get to the well first, before it dries up; where in the last analysis my responsibility is to myself alone, because in the end I am precisely that—alone. It shows up in cutthroat, take-no-prisoners practices in industry and sport, in economics and politics, in government and social life. Remember Ed Rollins, who managed the campaign for the current governor of New Jersey? "I'll do whatever it takes to win."

A second demon, terribly difficult to exorcise, is a way of thinking and living that turns sisters and brothers into unthinking or bitter enemies. I mean the racism that infects not only Ku Klux Klanners and skinheads, but in less obvious ways vast numbers of good ordinary people. We may have cleaned up our language; we may not discriminate legally; but the dislike, the hatred, bubbles beneath the surface, breaks out when jobs are at stake, when affirmative action moves onto our turf. Somewhat like the priest and Levite in Luke's parable of the Good Samaritan, white folk often "pass by on the other side" (Lk 10:31-32). Instinctively we are more afraid of blacks than of whites...or reds...or browns.

A third demon lodging in our tombs: consumerism. In actual living, so much of American society contradicts what Vatican II declared: "A person is more precious for what he or she is than for what he or she has."[2] Being rather than having.

Remember Lee Atwater, who almost singlehandedly turned the Bush campaign around in the late 80s? It took a deadly brain tumor to bring him to his senses, to let him see how immoral his lust for power and possessions had been, how pervasive such lust, how threatening to our country, how ultimately...empty.

Closer to your homes, listen to Linda Hargrove, head coach of the women's basketball team at Wichita State University. As quoted in your illustrious *Eagle* yesterday, she stated: "The whole approach to competition has changed. It's more materialistic. When I started coaching 22 years ago, I didn't have kids asking me what kind of shoes we wore or how many practice outfits we get. They were just thankful to have the opportunity to play. Now it's different."[3]

Little wonder that John Paul II could set side by side with the anguish and miseries of underdevelopment a contemporary super-development that

> makes people slaves of "possession" and of immediate gratifica-
> tion, with no other horizon than the multiplication or continual

replacement of the things already owned with others still better. This is the so-called civilization of "consumption" or "consumerism," which involves so much "throwing-away" and "waste".... To "have" objects and goods does not in itself perfect the human subject, unless it contributes to the maturing and enrichment of that subject's "being," that is to say unless it contributes to the realization of the human vocation as such.[4]

II

Second question: How can we drive these demons out? In the final analysis, of course, only God can drive out an insidious individualism, a rampant racism, a consuming consumerism. But God normally works through what philosophers call "secondary causes." More simply, God works through God's people. Through you and me. No homily can spell out adequately how, under God, you and I can destroy individualism, racism, and consumerism. For our purposes in this retreat/workshop, three suggestions.

First, before I preach the just Word to others, I must look into my own heart. Is biblical justice *my* way of living? Am I consistently faithful to my relationships: to God, to myself, to woman and man, to the earth? To the God who called me to this ministry of reconciliation? To the commitments *I* make freely day after day? To the men and women I have vowed to serve as Jesus served—even, therefore, unto crucifixion? To the earth, material things, nonhuman life, that I am summoned not to subdue but to use with reverence, with care, with love? Am I a man of community rather than a rugged individualist, indifferent to color or culture, concerned with being over having, sharing rather than possessing? Am I what I was created to be in God's eyes?

Second, am I ready to suffer for justice' sake? Not necessarily as the Salvadoran martyrs suffered—Archbishop Romero, the four American missionary women, the six Jesuits and their housekeeper with her daughter. Rather, does my mind ceaselessly struggle, agonize, sweat to grasp what biblical justice, God's justice, is all about? Am I prepared, like the Hebrew prophets, to bring to my people the raw challenge of God's justice, to face the indifference, the criticism, the dislike, the anger of my own people? Am I willing, like Jeremiah, to cry in frustration, "For 23 years I have spoken persistently to you, but you have not listened" (Jer 25:3)?

Third, do I realize, act on the conviction, that it is God who gives the increase? We priests, we preachers, can be tempted to a certain type of Pelagianism: We humans are the ones who make justice work, we who destroy rugged individualism, racism, consumerism. God does indeed need us, because God has chosen to need us. But grace—and justice, like peace, is a work of grace—grace is always and everywhere *God*-given. A source, I submit, of profound encouragement to us when the just Word seems just a word, with little power to change a culture, to transform human hearts. For, with St. Paul, we know that our strength lies not in what we have made of ourselves; our power rests in a Christ who was most powerful when he was crucified.

Today's Gospel closes with a conversation that merits our meditation. As Jesus is about to get into the boat that will take him to the other side of the lake, the man freed of his demons begs him, "Let me go with you." Surprisingly, Jesus says...no. "Go home to your friends, and tell them how much the Lord has done for you, and what mercy he has shown you" (Mk 5:18-19). A splendid way to preach the just Word: Go back to your people, tell them how much the Lord has done for *you*, how gracious he has been to *you*. *Be* your own just word.

Spiritual Life Center
Wichita, Kansas
January 31, 1994

11

ALL THINGS TO ALL PEOPLE
Fifth Sunday of the Year (B)

- 1 Corinthians 9:16-19, 22-23

"I have become all things to all people, that I might by all means save some."[1]

(1 Cor 9:22)

A remarkable remark, good friends. Remarkable for at least three reasons: the apostle who uttered it, the Lord who provoked it, and the Christians of today inspired by it. In consequence, three stages to my song and dance: (1) Paul, (2) Jesus, (3) you and I.

I

First, the apostle Paul who declared, "I have become all things to all people." Some facts from his life. That life was a remarkable wedding of good times and bad, of joy and sorrow. At times it reads like a thriller heaven-sent for a TV documentary. What did he look like? There is some reason to think he was short and bald, his beard was thick and his nose unmistakable, his eyebrows touched, his legs were, shall we say, curved. Still, people found him impressive; he was forceful, feisty, had fire in his belly, faced up fearlessly to Peter on circumcision.

But so much of his life was a paradox, so many seeming contradictions. With the Christians of Corinth he found himself weak, "in much fear and trembling" (1 Cor 2:3); in Asia Minor, "so utterly, unbearably crushed" that he "despaired of life itself" (2 Cor 1:8). On the other hand, he was caught up in ecstasy, "caught up into paradise"—such ecstasy that he "heard things that cannot be told,

51

which a human being may not utter" (2 Cor 12:2-4). He was stoned and
left for dead; riots rose up against him, plots to kill him; he was
shipwrecked three times, imprisoned in Jerusalem, in Caesarea, in
Rome. In his own moving confession, he was beaten more times than
he could count, was often near death, in danger from rivers and
robbers, in danger from Jews and Gentiles, in danger in the city and
the wilderness and at sea, in danger from false sisters and brothers, in
danger from hunger and thirst and cold, daily anxious for all the
churches (cf. 2 Cor 11:23-28). And yet, all through his letters, the words
"joyful," "happy," "delighted," "cheerful," "glad" run like a ceaseless
refrain. Joy was a profound reality in Paul's life, as profound as sorrow.

Paul's reaction to these realities? Very simply, "I have learned to
be content with whatever I have" (Phil 4:11). Content. Not like a cow
chewing its cud. Not indifferent, uninterested, neutral, unconcerned,
apathetic: "I couldn't care less." Not masochistic: "Hit me again, I like
it." It's an interesting Greek word Paul uses. It speaks of someone who
is independent, not enslaved to external events or other people, has
whatever he needs for peace and balance, is not the prey of each
passing wind, is not a Yo-yo manipulated by all sorts of jerks. Paul is his
own person.

The secret behind this reaction? Listen to him: "I know what it is
to have little, and I know what it is to have plenty. In any and all
circumstances I have learned the secret of facing fulness and hunger, of
having plenty and of being in need" (v. 12). He has "learned the
secret." Another remarkable Greek word. As in the great mystery
religions, Paul possesses the secret. And what is that? "I can do all
things in him who gives me strength" (v. 13). This is not the proud
independence, the utter self-sufficiency, of the Stoics. Paul relies totally
on, is intimately one with, one other, an unseen power. His independence he acquires not by separating himself from others, but by joining
himself to Christ. All things are his, but only in so far as he is Christ's,
and because Christ is God's. The Lord has initiated him into what
Protestant theologian Karl Barth translated as "the mystery of life with
its ups and downs of having and being without."[2]

II

Such is the man who writes to the Christians of Corinth, "I have
made myself a slave to all, so that I might win more of them.... To the
weak I became weak, so that I might win the weak. I have become all
things to all people, that I might by all means save some" (1 Cor 9:19-
25). This is not the shrewd politician: "I know what you're going

through; I had to work in a deli to get through high school." This is not an earlier Ed Rollins, campaign manager for the new governor of New Jersey, with his blatant "My mission, when I'm hired by someone, is to do whatever it takes to win."[3] No, this is the man who exclaimed, "I have been crucified with Christ; and it is no longer I who live, but it is Christ who lives in me. And the life I now live in the flesh I live by faith in the Son of God, who loved me and gave himself for me" (Gal 2:19-20). This is a man who loved each of his sisters and brothers so intensely that, after the example of Christ, he wanted to experience what they experienced.

After the example of Christ. For this is what Jesus did. The Son of God took our flesh not because he had to. He took our flesh because he wanted to *experience* as a man what he already *knew* as God. He wanted to experience the way we live just as we experience it. Not abstractly, intellectually; no, concretely, in quivering flesh. And so he was born as we are born, of a woman's body. To escape death at Herod's hands, he fled with Mary and Joseph to Egypt the way men, women, and children flee in terror from Bosnia and Haiti. He who had shaped heaven and earth with a word learned from Joseph how to turn out a plow. He who was Love without a beginning learned from Mary how to love God. He touched the rotting flesh of lepers, fingered the eyes of the blind, laid his hand on Peter's feverish mother-in-law. He experienced what it feels like to have his townspeople fling him over a cliff, his fellow Jews shout he had a devil, his relatives suggest he was mad. He experienced what it feels like when one of your intimate friends sells you for silver, betrays you with a kiss; when another who had walked with him for three years denied to a servant girl that he had ever looked into Jesus' eyes; when only one of the Twelve stood with his mother beneath the cross. He wanted to experience what it feels like to die...what you and I feel when we know the next breath may be our last.

This is precisely what St. Paul wanted to do. He wanted not only to know with his sharp intellect, he wanted to experience what it feels like to be so terribly weak in body that you'd rather be dead; what it feels like to be so dreadfully weak in spirit that you don't do the good you know you ought to do, you do the very evil you know you should not do. He wanted to experience what it feels like to be afraid: in prison, on a storm-tossed sea, on a city's streets; to be afraid of other so-called Christians. He wanted to sense in his flesh what it feels like to be "cold as hell," to hunger for the scraps of food the wealthy might throw him, to have his throat desert-dry from thirst. In a word, he wanted to share the kind of life lived by anyone and everyone he met, here, there, everywhere. The kind of life God-in-flesh lived. And he did. He did indeed.

Why? By all that is human and sensible, why? Not because he liked to suffer. He did not. Remember how he told the Christians of Corinth, "a thorn was given me in the flesh, a messenger of Satan to torment me, to keep me from being too flushed with success" (2 Cor 12:7)? We are not sure what the thorn was: perhaps a hiatal hernia, perhaps a deep depression, perhaps the hostility of his enemies. Whatever it was, did he say, "More, Lord, pile it on"? No. "Three times I appealed to the Lord about this, that it would leave me" (v. 8). Paul wanted to experience the lot of the less fortunate "so that I might save some" (1 Cor 9:22). "I do it all for the sake of the gospel" (v. 23). He wanted to bring them to Christ.

III

Now Paul and Jesus lead directly to my third point: What of you and me? Frankly, I stand here before you profoundly humbled. Why? Because I stand before men and women who are living day by day the kind of life Jesus said makes us worthy of the kingdom he preached: "I was hungry and you gave me food, I was thirsty and you gave me something to drink, I was a stranger and you welcomed me, I was naked and you gave me clothing, I was sick and you took care of me, I was in prison and you visited me." For, "as you did it to one of the least of these my sisters and brothers, you did it to me" (Mt 25:35-36, 40). I am humbled, too, because I stand before some of these very sisters and brothers in whom you recognize the crucified face of Jesus.

If I were asked to portray in living color that striking scene in Matthew's Gospel, I would begin by painting your ecumenical Stewpot.[4] Food for the flesh indeed: two million meals in two decades. But more than that, for you touch not only empty stomachs but the whole human frame: mouths in pain from rotting teeth, nerves convulsed with drink or drugs, bones aching for shelter against blazing sun and chilling frost, hearts hungry for work with dignity, minds numbed by sheer emptiness, the vulnerable young and the shriveled aging. You give the crucified images of Christ reason to hope that tomorrow may be different, a bit more human. And most importantly, like Paul, what stimulates all this is love. So terribly important; for, as the apostle of charity Vincent de Paul insisted over three centuries ago, "Unless you love, the poor will never forgive you for the bread you give them."

In your corporate activity as the Body of Christ, you live the sentence of Paul that triggered this sermon: "I have become all things to all people." Yes, to all people, whatever their belief or unbelief. In this you remind me of an insightful remark made recently within my Roman Catholic community. At a meeting of our incredibly far-ranging Catholic Charities, a gentleman with 16 years of Catholic education asked a speaker: "Why do we provide this phenomenal array of services to so many millions of people? We never ask them what they believe, whether they practice their religion, never even ask them whether they are Catholic." The reply from the speaker? "We don't act this way because *they* are Catholic, but because *we* are Catholic." You know, you can broaden that response: "We don't act the way we do because *they* are *Christian*, but because *we* are *Christian*." Because, like Jesus, our mission is to the whole human family, to every male and female the Lord created, to each person from Adam to Antichrist for whom the Son of God was born in Bethlehem, for whom he poured out his blood one dark afternoon outside Jerusalem.

You may say to me, "But what about that last phrase of Paul, 'that I might *save* some'"? Salvation is indeed a profoundly spiritual reality: oneness with God now and for ever. But I believe committed Presbyterians can in conscience echo the strong language of the 1974 Synod of Catholic Bishops:

> Human dignity is rooted in the image and reflection of God in each of us. It is this which makes all persons essentially equal. The integral development of persons makes more clear the divine image in them. In our time the Church has grown more deeply aware of this truth; hence she believes firmly that the promotion of human rights is required by the gospel and is central to her ministry.[5]

Very simply, our covenant in Christ's blood includes *two* inseparable commandments: "Love God with all your heart" and "Love your neighbor as yourself" (Mt 22:37, 39). Not a psychological command, "Love the other as much or as little as you love yourself." That could be a dangerous standard for genuine love. The commandment means, "Love your sisters and brothers as if you were standing in their shoes." In fact, this is Jesus' commandment: "Love one another as I have loved you" (Jn 15:12). Love them even unto crucifixion.

Dear sisters and brothers in Christ: I can close no more fittingly than by repeating the words of a Missouri rabbi after he had helped serve lunch to 400 people at the Stewpot:

> As I looked into the faces of those to whom I served water, and as they looked into mine, a voice with me spoke saying, "Behold, God is in this place. God's face shines in the faces of those who

gratefully give and gratefully receive. You made a difference today. You showed these people respect. You gave them hope. Give thanks to God and praise God's name."[6]

First Presbyterian Church
Dallas, Texas
February 6, 1994

12
SACRIFICE YOUR OWN SON?
Thirteenth Week of the Year, Thursday (A)

• Genesis 22:1-19
• Matthew 9:1-8

Back in the days of Enlightenment humanism, Emmanuel Kant inveighed against a so-called command of God that would order a father to slay his own son: "There are certain cases in which [you] can be convinced that it cannot be God whose voice [you] think [you] hear: when the voice commands [you] to do what is opposed to the moral law, though the phenomenon seems to [you] ever so majestic and surpassing the whole of nature, [you] must count it a deception."¹ In that context I suggest that we ask two questions: (1) What did today's first reading mean then? (2) What might it be saying to you and me now? Very simply, let's mull over Abraham and ourselves.²

I

First, Abraham. Intrigued though I am by Kant's conviction, a homily is not the place to argue the morality of God's startling command to Abraham, "Take your son, your only son Isaac, whom you love, and slay him in sacrifice" (Gen 22:2). Oh yes, it's a fascinating topic for sacerdotal discussion some disenchanted evening—together with other engaging moral topics like the 700 wives and 300 concubines of Solomon, or Abraham himself telling Pharaoh that Sarah was his sister to save his own skin. But here—here we begin with a fact: God is testing Abraham.

It is the tenth of Abraham's trials, and the most difficult. Put yourself in Abraham's sandals. He has received the Lord's solemn promise: Of his loins a great nation, a host of nations, will be born. And he believes—even when Sarah is childless; believes into the unbelievable day when Sarah pushing 91 conceives Isaac, with the assistance of centenarian Abraham. And now—now God is about to take from Abraham the most credible proof of God's fidelity: the son who is to realize God's promise of a great nation, the Isaac destined by God to continue Abraham's line. Not only will Isaac die, he through whom the great nation is to be, he who is still but a boy. Abraham himself is commanded to slay him, to destroy God's solemn promise. How can he still believe?

A masterpiece of biblical narrative. On the one hand, a God whose demands are absolute, whose will is beyond human understanding. On the other hand, a man with glaring human weaknesses, buoyed only by God's promises, promises that to all human appearances are about to be shattered. His response? In the face of such a God, a command so ruthless, so unlike the God of the covenant, the founder of Israel reveals his incredible character. No protest; only trust. He entrusts to his God his whole life, the future of his family, the great nation God has promised. "Here I am" (Gen 22:1). In fact, this biblical affirmation of utter availability is uttered before any command is given. And it remains even when an angel stays his hand: "Now I know how devoted you are to God, since you have not withheld your son, your only son, from me" (v. 12).

II

And what of you and me? We too have been privileged with promises—God's promises. Breath-taking promises. Promises that are linked to the covenant that is the New Testament. Christ's covenant with us, sealed with his blood: "I am with you always" (Mt 28:20). "The gates of hell will not prevail against" my church (Mt 16:18). "I will see you again, and your hearts will rejoice, and your joy no one will take from you" (Jn 16:22). "Believe in me and you will move mountains, cast out demons, speak in new tongues, pick up snakes, nothing deadly will hurt you, you will lay hands on the sick and they will recover" (Mt 17:20; Mk 16:17-18). "Stop worrying over what you are to eat, drink, wear. Strive first for the kingdom of God, and all these will be given to you as well" (Mt 6:31, 33). "Speak the word with boldness" (Acts 4:29) and your enemies will not be able to withstand you. "The kingdom of God has come near" (Mk 1:15), is among you, is within your community.

But where are these promises now? Christ with us always? Hell will not prevail? Tell that to the Catholics in China loyal to Rome. Your joy no one will take from you? Tell that to a mother cradling her dead baby in the devastation of Bosnia. Believe and you will move mountains? Preach that to the homeless and the hungry, to the drug-addicted and the AIDS-afflicted. Stop worrying over tomorrow? Mumble those words to the 150 million children who will die this decade. Speak the word with boldness? What of you who can complain with Jeremiah, "For 23 years the word of the Lord has come to me, and I have spoken persistently to you, but you have not listened" (Jer 25:3)? The kingdom is near, is among us? Listen to our Jewish sisters and brothers: "We can see no kingdom, no peace, no redemption."

Our response? Like Abraham, not to question God's fidelity to God's promises. We begin with a fact: God...is...faithful. It is not a truth that is born of a syllogism, of rigid philosophical demonstration. It is not a truth that surges up from the ceaseless experience of humankind. It is a truth we trumpet because, like Abraham, we have been gifted. Gifted with what? Gifted with trust—a God-given confidence that, no matter what happens, God will be there, with us, for us. It is the constant cry of the Psalmist:

> You who live in the shelter of the Most High,
>   who abide in the shadow of the Almighty,
> will say to the Lord, "My refuge and my fortress;
>   my God, in whom I trust."
>
> (Ps 91:1-2)

Here the problem is not so much *God's* fidelity as *my* fidelity. Mother Teresa was so accurately on target: "God asks not that I be successful but that I be faithful." The neuralgic question is, "How faithful am I?" Here is where fidelity and justice kiss. For biblical justice is fidelity to responsibilities, to relationships, particularly those that stem from a covenant with God. I who dare to preach the just Word, how do I live it? This on four levels. (1) My relationship to God. I mean a profound oneness with Father, Son, and Holy Spirit. I mean my prayer life, my spirituality, my readiness to respond "Here I am," no matter what the Lord asks of me, even the Isaac that symbolizes my most precious possession, my treasured ideas of how I should serve God. (2) My relationship to myself. I mean the schizophrenia Paul agonized over, the split in my inner self, Paul's "I do not understand my own actions. For I do not do what I want, but I do the very thing I hate" (Rom 7:15). (3) My relationship to sisters and brothers. I mean the second great commandment of the law and the gospel, the love Jesus said "is like" loving God (Mt 22:38): doing unto others as I would want them to do unto me, as God has done unto me. (4) My relationship to the earth. I mean the way I relate to what is not human: the earth that nourishes me, the "things" I eat and drink and wear and use, the "waste" in my life.

In brief, what might you and I learn from Abraham? How to focus not on God's justice but on our own. Extraordinarily important for priests who must preach biblical justice, must rage against irresponsible relationships, must challenge unjust "habits of the heart" in our society and in our church.

The problem is, such a focus calls for crucifixion. To live justly on those four levels, I must sacrifice. I must be ready, like Abraham, to put the knife to so much that is dear to me: my will on earth, my way of running the Church of Christ, my plans for the perfect parish, my personal comfort, my desire to be liked and loved and praised and applauded, my yearning for years of tireless energy and good health in the service of Christ and his people, my dreams for the years that lie ahead.

Three momentous monosyllables are crucial here—the terribly difficult declaration that characterized Abraham and Jesus, the total commitment that must distinguish everyone who is called to preach justice: "Here...I...am." In the context of my experience of priesthood, in the light of my summons to preach and live the just Word, dare I declare it this evening with fresh, unparalleled conviction: "Here I am, Lord"? If I can, then surely the day will dawn when not an angel but my very God will say to me, "Now I know how devoted you are to me, since you have not withheld from me all that you love most."

Holy Family Retreat House
Hampton, Virginia
July 1, 1993

13

HE TOOK, HE BLESSED, HE BROKE, HE GAVE
Eighteenth Week of the Year, Monday (B)

- Jeremiah 28:1-17
- Matthew 14:13-21

As I mused over today's Gospel, three words particularly important for contemporary preachers[1] gradually came to mind, slowly came into focus: multiplication, Eucharist, and justice. Multiplication will be quite obvious; Eucharist calls for some searching, researching; and justice simply begs for reflection on its relation to Eucharist. So then, a word on each word.

I

The first word is...multiplication. Jesus somehow multiplied five loaves so that five thousand men, plus uncounted women and children, could satisfy their hunger. You know, Scripture scholars have had huge fun, played exciting games, battered unyielding walls here.[2] Here is the only miracle from the public ministry of Jesus that all four evangelists narrate. The accounts are so alike that the question naturally arises: Who copied from whom? And since both Matthew and Mark have two multiplication accounts, one for five thousand men and the other for four thousand, are these separate incidents or simply variations of the same incident? If we settle for two accounts of the same multiplication, which is the older?

Since a homily is not a lecture, a pulpit not a classroom, we can leave these questions for some disenchanted evening. We can assume one multiplication, and live with the account we have just heard, Matthew's first account.

On the sheer face of it, it is a touching story. It reveals Jesus withdrawing by boat to a deserted place after hearing of John the

Baptist's beheading. To mourn? To pray? To rest? We are not told. We do know that large crowds followed him on foot. Out of curiosity? To listen? To be healed? We are not told. We *are* told that when Jesus saw them, "he had compassion for them and cured their sick" (Mt 14:14). We *are* told that the sun was close to setting, that the disciples were worried about people hunger, that they urged Jesus to send all of them away to the nearest delis so they could buy lox and bagels for themselves. We *are* told that to their surprise Jesus said, "They don't have to go away; *you* give them something to eat" (v. 16). We *are* told that the disciples faced Jesus with some basic culinary facts: five loaves and two fishes. We *are* told that, despite this baffling reality, Jesus told the thousands to sit down on the grass, that he broke the five loaves, gave them to the disciples to distribute; that every man, woman, and child had his or her fill; that enough was left over to fill 12 baskets.

Matthew does not tell us what John relates. This miracle caused people to say, "This is undoubtedly the Prophet" we've been expecting (Jn 6:14). And Jesus "fled back to the mountain alone" because he sensed they would "carry him off to make him king" (v. 15). As Matthew had learned it, Jesus did three things: He told the disciples to row to the other side; he sent the crowds away; he "went up the mountain by himself to pray" (Mt 14:23).

II

The second word is...Eucharist. Why did Jesus multiply five loaves to feed the hungry thousands? An obvious answer is a sentence early on in today's Gospel: "He saw a great crowd, and he had compassion for them" (v. 14). The Greek word is a word that pervades the Gospels, a word constantly used of Jesus, a word that tells of sympathy and mercy and love, stemming from the deepest recesses of the human person. And surely the Jesus who had compassion for the sick, for a leper, for two blind men, for a father and his epileptic boy, for a mother who had lost her only son, surely he had compassion for men, women, and children who had "followed him on foot" (v. 13) for miles, had listened to him "teach them many things" (Mk 6:34), and now were aching for food. In fact, Mark has Jesus saying, "I have compassion for the crowd, *because* they have been with me now for three days and have nothing to eat. If I send them away hungry to their homes, they will faint on the way—and some of them have come from a great distance" (Mk 8:2-3).[3]

A significant segment of the story, without doubt; but also without doubt, not the whole story. Mark tells us that the disciples "did not understand about the loaves" (Mk 6:52). Surely they had no trouble understanding Jesus' compassion, his sympathy, his mercy, his love; they had experienced it, even in their own regard. What was it they failed to understand?

Here the story gets more and more exciting. As you know, the miracles of Jesus were handed down by word of mouth in the early Christian communities; they were told and retold in the Sunday assemblies, meditated, relished, long before the Gospels were written as we have them. As the story of the loaves and fishes was passed along, Christians were increasingly struck by a startling similarity. They saw more and more clearly that there must be a close connection between the multiplication of loaves and a central Christian mystery. I mean... the Eucharist.

Put yourself in early Christian shoes. Recall what each priest says and does when he re-enacts the Last Supper, when he consecrates the bread and feeds the people with the body of Christ: Jesus took bread, blessed it, broke it, and gave it to his disciples. Now listen to Matthew at the multiplication: "Taking the five loaves and the two fish,...he blessed and broke the loaves, and gave them to the disciples, and the disciples gave them to the crowds" (Mt 14:19). He took, he blessed, he broke, he gave.

Coincidence? Hardly. Not that the multiplication was the Eucharist. But the Gospels see the multiplication as a sign. It looked back and it looked ahead. It fulfilled the Prior Testament promises that in the days to come God would feed God's people with plenty. Take Isaiah. Promising the exiles from Babylon a new exodus, Isaiah echoes the words of the Lord:

> They shall feed along the ways,
> on all bare heights shall be their pasture;
> they shall not hunger or thirst.
>
> (Isa 49:9-10)

And the multiplication looked forward to the Last Supper and all subsequent Suppers, when Christ would feed his sisters and brothers with the true bread from heaven, the bread that makes it possible for us to live for ever: "This is the bread that comes down from heaven, so that one may eat of it and not die.... The bread that I will give for the life of the world is my flesh" (Jn 6:50-51).

III

The third word is...justice. Not simply or primarily ethical justice: Give to each man, woman, and child what is due to them, what they

deserve. Rather, biblical justice: fidelity to relationships, to responsibilities, especially as these stem from our covenant cut in the blood of
Christ. Not only loving the Lord our God with all our heart and soul,
all our mind and strength. Loving each sister and brother as another
"I," as if we were standing in their shoes. And caring lovingly for all
God's creation, for the earth on which we humans dance so lightly and
which we rape so thoughtlessly.

But how does the Eucharist touch justice? I myself begin with a
principle that has been central to Catholic theology and was
reaffirmed by Vatican II:

> The liturgy is the summit toward which the Church's activity is
> directed; at the same time it is the source from which all her power
> proceeds.... The renewal in the Eucharist of the Lord's covenant
> with humans draws the faithful into the compelling love of Christ
> and sets them afire. From the liturgy, therefore, especially from
> the Eucharist, as from a fountain, grace is channeled into us, and
> that sanctification of men and women in Christ and the
> glorification of God, to which all other activities of the Church
> stretch and strain as toward their goal, are most effectively
> achieved.[4]

Here Vatican II echoes Leo XIII's strong affirmation, "From the
Eucharist the Church draws and possesses all its vigor and glory, all the
gifts with which God has embellished it, all the blessings it has."[5]

If that is so, then a spirituality of biblical justice must be a
Eucharistic spirituality. More than any other influence, the Real
Presence of the whole Christ in the Eucharist makes it possible for you
and me to be eucharists (small e). I mean *really present* to our brothers
and sisters, particularly to the poor and the oppressed. A presence of
the whole person, not only mind and money but hand and heart, flesh
and spirit, emotions and passions. A presence that, like Christ's,
springs from love and leads to love: "Love one another as I have loved
you" (Jn 15:12).

To deepen that spirituality, mull ceaselessly over the four words
that dominate both the multiplication of loaves and the Last Supper:
Jesus took, Jesus blessed, Jesus broke, Jesus gave. As Jesus *took* bread, so
he took you and me, chose you and me to follow him ever so intimately,
to be servants of God's justice, to be living examples of fidelity to
relationships, to inspire fidelity to responsibilities. As Jesus *blessed* the
bread, changing it at the Supper into the incarnate Son of God, so his
baptismal blessing changed us into agents of the reconciling Christ,
sent us forth to fuse into one the scattered children of God. As Jesus
broke the bread, so he breaks us, destroys the false self in us, transforms

the "I" in the fire of suffering; for "Unless the grain of wheat falls into the earth and dies, it remains just a single grain," cannot produce images of itself, "but if it dies, it bears much fruit" (Jn 12:24). And as Jesus *gave* the bread, so he gives you and me, gives us to his people for their hungers, gives us to the world for its life.[6]

In this context I find it stimulating to reimagine the recessional of each Mass all over the world. It is not an ending; it is a fresh beginning. It is our movement, the movement of our people, from church to world, from altar to people, from Christ crucified on Calvary to Christ crucified on our crossroads. "This is *my* body, and it is given for *you*."

Cardinal Stritch Retreat House
Mundelein, Illinois
August 1, 1994

14

SHOULD YOU NOT HAVE HAD MERCY?
Twenty-fourth Sunday of the Year (A)

- Sirach 27:30–28:7
- Romans 14:7-9
- Matthew 18:21-35

Today's Gospel opens with one of Peter's straight-on questions: "Lord, if my brother sins against me, how often should I forgive him? As many as seven times?" (Mt 18:21). Now there's a background to Peter's question.[1] You see, Peter thought he was being quite generous. For a good reason. In rabbinic teaching a man had to forgive his brother *three* times—but no more. For this the rabbis went back to the opening chapters of the prophet Amos. There *God's* forgiveness apparently extends to three offenses; come the fourth offense, God punishes. Since no one may be more gracious than God, the rabbis concluded, our own forgiveness may not extend beyond three offenses.

So, big-hearted Peter doubles the rabbis plus one: How about seven, Lord? And he settles back with a little smile of satisfaction. Surely the Lord will pat him on the back for generosity beyond the call of duty, generosity on Jesus' own level. To his surprise, Jesus is not impressed: "Not seven times but, I tell you, 77 times"[2] (v. 22). In other words, you may not attach a number, a limit, to the times you forgive.

A powerful response, isn't it? Yes, but it raises profound questions. (1) Is Jesus really serious? (2) If he is, what lies behind so extravagant a response to Peter? (3) How does this touch you and me, touch a genuinely Christian spirituality?[3]

I

First, is Jesus really serious? No limit to forgiveness? No point at which you say to an offending man or woman, "Enough! I've had it up to here"? Is Jesus actually asking the Muslims in Bosnia to forgive the

Serbs who ravish their land and their women? Asking the black man to forgive the three young whites who poured gasoline on him and set him ablaze? Asking a father to forgive a beast who brutalized his little daughter? Asking Mr. Weinstein to forgive the characters who buried him alive for 12 days?[4] Asking Pope John Paul to forgive his would-be assassin? Asking us to forgive every Judas who has ever betrayed us? Asking me to forgive the Salvadoran soldiers who massacred six of my brother Jesuits? Asking the Jews to forgive the German butchers who gassed their parents in Auschwitz? Six million executions, six million pardons?

Here two important observations. First, recall what Peter is asking: "If my brother sins against me...."[5] Peter is talking about a personal offense committed by one member of the community against another member of the community; he is not asking for a comprehensive treatise on all possible offenses, no matter by whom or against whom. The questions I just asked are legitimate, but Peter is asking about offenses by fellow believers, and that is the context of Jesus' reply.

Second observation: In traditional Jesuit style, I make a crucial distinction. An American Scripture scholar teaching in Africa put it with admirable conciseness—about as pithily, as briefly and forcefully, as I have ever heard it. He distinguished two strong monosyllables: crime and sin. And he said, "You punish crime; you forgive sin."[6] John Paul II tenderly held the hand that held the gun, forgave Mehmet Ali Agca; he did not ask the Italian government to release him from prison. No society dare release dangerous criminals; not to punish criminal violation of the social order is to court disaster. And still Jesus can say, "Forgive them. Forgive the sin within the crime."

Despite those two brilliant observations, problems remain. For Jesus did not limit forgiveness to members of his community. He explained the forgiveness in the Our Father with a strong sentence: "If you do not forgive others, neither will your Father forgive your trespasses" (Mt 6:14). And even if we see the difference between crime and sin, what can it possibly mean to forgive another's sin? Jesus is indeed serious, but to understand this a bit better, move on to my second question.

II

What lies behind Jesus' extravagant response to Peter? If I want to understand it, I must begin not with man or woman but with God. For forgiveness begins with God. You heard the responsorial psalm so movingly hymned by the choir:

> The Lord is merciful and gracious,
>> slow to anger and abounding in steadfast love....
> [The Lord] does not deal with us according to our sins,
>> nor requite us according to our iniquities....
> As far as the east is from the west,
>> so far does [the Lord] remove our transgressions from us.
>
> (Ps 103:8, 10, 12)

The Old Testament surprises many a Catholic. Indeed, the wrath of God is there; but more pervasive than wrath is God's love. It is unforgettably enshrined in Isaiah, when despairing Jews complained, "The Lord has forsaken me, my Lord has forgotten me." And the Lord replied:

> Can a woman forget her nursing child,
>> or show no compassion for the child of her womb?
> Even these may forget,
>> yet I will not forget you.
> See, I have inscribed you on the palms of my hands.
>
> (Isa 49:14–16a)

Love divine was revealed most strikingly in Yahweh's compassion: Yahweh is a God of forgiveness. If you were fascinated by the film "The Fugitive," starring an innocent Harrison Ford, read the Hebrew Testament, starring a not so innocent Israel. In a sense, it is the story of a fugitive. But this time the fugitive is a people; that people is time and again fleeing from God, refusing God's love, the refusal of love we call sin. Not only individuals: Solomon with his foreign women, 700 wives and 300 concubines, so that "his wives turned away his heart after other gods; and his heart was not true to the Lord his God" (1 Kgs 11:4). The people by and large. In captivity—Egypt and Babylon; in the desert, worshiping a golden calf and complaining of God's menu. Isaiah has to summon the people to national repentance; for lies, injustice, violence, slaughter of the innocent add up to a denial of God, have "made a separation," raised "barriers," between the whole community and its Lord (Isa 59:2).

But time and again, against all the odds, God's love reaches out to them. In the midst of their despair, God's call:

> Arise, shine! For your light has come,
>> and the glory of the Lord has risen upon you....
> Your people shall all be righteous,
>> and your God will be your glory.
>
> (Isa 60:1, 21a)

God never stopped offering love; all God asked was that Israel accept God's love, agree to love anew. Call it contrition, confession, conversion—the Israelites simply had to allow themselves to love. Now even this was beyond a sinner's native power. So what did God do? Listen to the Lord in Ezekiel: "A new heart I will give you, and a new spirit I will put within you" (Ezek 36:26). This God does, because to pardon is characteristic of God: "Thou sparest all things, for they are thine, O Lord who lovest the living" (Wis 11:26).

Is it any wonder that the Jewish sage who wrote the book called Sirach wrote, "Forgive your neighbor the wrong he has done, and then your sins will be pardoned when you pray" (Sir 28:2)?

For Christians, this message of love comes incarnate in Jesus, is inscribed in his flesh. "God so loved the world" that God gave the world, gave you and me, not some avenging angel to cleanse our hearts with a heavenly Tide, but God's own Son, "so that everyone who believes in him may not perish but have eternal life" (Jn 3:16). And what sort of forgiveness did that involve? Listen to today's parable; it's highly important.

You see, the first servant owed his master "10,000 talents"; the second servant owed his fellow servant "100 denarii." Let's get concrete. A talent was worth 15 years' wages for a laborer; a denarius, one day's wages. So then, 10,000 talents? 150,000 working days. A hundred denarii? One hundred working days. Servant number 1 put his fellow servant in prison for a measly three months' wages; the generous master forgave a debt his servant would have had to work 410 years to pay off.

Remember, the master in the parable is God. We humans have been forgiven a debt so enormous that we could never pay for it: the debt which sin, enmity with God, hangs on us. Nothing any man or woman can do to us can compare with that debt. Nothing that we can forgive compares even faintly with what we have been forgiven: the sin that brought about the death of God's only Son. To pay the debt that we owed, the Son of God was crucified. Is it any wonder Jesus says there should be no limit to our willingness to forgive?

III

Our willingness to forgive—this introduces my third point. We are asked by Jesus to forgive others as God forgives us, to live the Our Father, "Forgive us our trespasses as we forgive those who trespass against us." But what does it mean for God to forgive me? It does not mean that God forgets what I have done; it does not mean that my sin is no longer a fact, is wiped out of history. For God, to forgive me is to change me. Through God's grace, at the very roots of my being I have a new relationship with God. My whole being is alive with the life of God; Father, Son, and Holy Spirit live within me. Their love courses through me, and I—I am in love again. Not just in word; I am incredibly one with God. I am St. Paul's "new creature," a "new creation" (2 Cor 5:17).

Only God can forgive like that—a forgiveness where the words "I forgive you" tell the offender that he or she is different, has been changed, transformed from enemy to friend. Then what is left for us? It is indeed God who changes hearts, but men and women, you and I, can be God's instruments. How?

Our task is like John the Baptist's: We go before the Lord to prepare his way, to pave the way for his coming. A highly pertinent example. Nine years ago, I preached at the University of Notre Dame on this same Sunday. I said that, when Pope John Paul murmured to his would-be assassin "I forgive you," we could not say that Agca was changed within, we did not know. But a year after the pope's visit we did know. Agca

> proclaimed that he was renouncing terrorism to become a man of peace.... He traced his transformation to a prison visit with the pope last year.... After close reading of the Koran, Agca said, he had become a devout Muslim with "profound respect" for Christianity. And he promised that if he were freed, he would become "a preacher, going to all nations of the world preaching good and the truth to all people."[7]

It was not the pope who changed the heart of Agca; it was the Lord. We simply prepare the way. But we are awfully important. But only if we prepare the way with love. Not with earth-shaking pronouncements like Jesus' bloody cry from the cross, "Father, forgive them" (Lk 23:34). Not able to resolve all the problems that offenses and forgiveness raise. Rather how we react to the everyday incidents that tear us from one another: the harsh word spoken by wife or husband in anger; the stubborn human streak that keeps me from taking the first step because I'm the one who was wronged; the hardness in my heart toward those who robbed me of the Latin Mass; the dislike in my bones for those who select the hymns I have to sing; the hatred in my heart for conservatives or liberals, for those who don't think as clearly as I do, the obnoxious office manager or the absentee landlord; a three-point homilist....

There are two remarkable benefits that come from forgiving. A first benefit touches us who forgive: "If you forgive others their trespasses, your heavenly Father will also forgive you" (Mt 6:14). Not a bad exchange. A second benefit accrues to those we forgive: We can be instruments of God's grace to others, help make them better than they are. And isn't this our vocation as Christians? You and I can apply to ourselves what St. Paul says of himself:

> God reconciled us to Himself through Christ, and has given us the ministry of reconciliation, that is, in Christ God was reconciling the world to Himself, not counting their trespasses against them, and entrusting the message of reconciliation to us. So we are ambassadors for Christ, since God is making His appeal through us....
>
> (2 Cor 5:18–20a)

Let me sum up the heart of the matter. There are two quite different approaches to offense and forgiveness, to reconciliation. One approach is the usual human approach; the other is the Christian approach that goes back to Jesus. In the usual approach, I offend you unjustly—say, tell lies about you, ruin your reputation; you expect me to discover how wrong I was, expect me to repent, expect me to say that I'm sorry, that I will repair the injury; then you forgive me. In the Christian understanding of reconciliation, the process is reversed. You have experienced how much God has freely forgiven you; aware of that, with God's grace you forgive me for what I have done to you; inspired by your forgiveness, I repent of my lying and begin to rebuild my Christian existence. Reconciliation begins not with me, the offender; reconciliation begins with you, the victim.[8]

Difficult? Terribly difficult. I cannot claim it is always possible; I simply claim this is what the God of forgiveness holds out to us as "the way to go." For in this way we carry on the reconciling work of Christ; for without our collaboration reconciliation with God will rarely happen. And without reconciliation with God there is no redemption, no salvation. Men and women are brought closer and closer to Christ to the extent that we link our arms to the crucified Christ and murmur, "Father, forgive them...."

Holy Trinity Church
Washington, D.C.
September 12, 1993

15

NO LOVE, NO EUCHARIST
Twenty-fourth Week of the Year, Monday (B)

- 1 Corinthians 11:17-26, 33
- Luke 7:1-10

Some time ago I read a riveting report from a priest in Calcutta. He had been invited to offer Mass for Mother Teresa and her community at their House of the Dying. When the time came for Holy Communion, he felt deeply how honored he was to be giving Communion to this small, intense woman clothed in sari and sandals. Suddenly he abandoned that line of thinking—abandoned it when he saw the way she looked at the consecrated Host. It was then he realized that the genuine wonder of the moment was not that he was giving Holy Communion to a living saint, but that he was holding in his hand the body of Christ.

But that was only part of the story. The priest went on to tell of Mother Teresa's powerful faith. Mother Teresa, he said, believes in two kinds of "real presence." With the eyes of faith she sees the living Christ under the appearances of bread and wine; and with the eyes of faith she also sees the same living Christ in the people she serves so tenderly, so lovingly. "Mother Teresa," he wrote, "is a believer. Christ is always there for her in each of the broken and miserable people she ministers to. She reverences them as she does the consecrated Eucharist."

In that context let me begin with St. Paul and his Corinthian Christians, move briskly to Mother Teresa and her broken people, and end with you and me.[1]

I

First, Paul. Paul is angry. When the Christians of Corinth come together in a private home to celebrate the Eucharist, to his way of thinking there is no Eucharist. Even though the ritual words are uttered, there is no Eucharist. Why? Because there is no love. There is only division. The wealthier come early, eat their own supper, leave nothing for the poor who have been working all day. "One goes hungry and another becomes drunk" (1 Cor 11:21). Because the Eucharistic food is the Lord, you violate its sacred character, you violate the Lord's presence, by selfish individualism, by disregarding the poor. No Eucharist because no community.[2]

Canon lawyers may shout "But it's valid," theologians might echo their protest. But Paul is not interested in our precious validity; he is concerned for a Eucharist that is fruitful, a Eucharist that is a sharing in God's grace. But...no love, no grace. No grace, no Eucharist.

II

Second, Mother Teresa. Not a theologian, but a woman with incredible insight, unbelievable ability to break through the tortuous stammerings of us theologians and live the wondrous realities we struggle to express. To her, one sentence says it all: "This is my body that is [broken] for you" (v. 24). Teresa has grasped, has been grasped by, the Eucharistic reality that makes sense of her life. The body of Christ that is the Eucharist is not a private party, a me-and-Jesus two-step. The body of Christ that is the Eucharist makes the Body of Christ that is the Church. It is broken not to satisfy isolated individuals but to build community. It is broken particularly for those who are themselves uncommonly broken, who share more of Jesus' crucifixion than of his resurrection. That body is broken and given even for those who have not the joy of receiving it.

Teresa grasps and lives the two facets of Eucharistic belief that Catholic spirituality stresses today, has actually always stressed. (1) Christ is really present in what looks like bread, feels like bread, tastes like bread but is not bread, is simply and truly Christ Jesus our Lord. (2) The same Christ is really present in every man, woman, and child no matter how inhuman; for each has been shaped in the image of Christ, a likeness to Christ that even sin cannot utterly destroy. The 50,000 bodies Teresa and her sisters have brought into their home to die with dignity— each was carried in because he or she is Christ, a Christ crucified.

III

Third, what of you and me? Each day we are privileged to transmute wheat and wine into the risen Christ. Not simply or even primarily for ourselves; not even simply for our parishioners. This Bread, Jesus said, is given "for the life of the world" (Jn 6:33, 51). Each Eucharistic recessional is not an end but a beginning. It is a movement from church to world, from altar to people, from Christ crucified on Calvary to Christ crucified on the highways and byways of our world.

For us and for our people, for those who struggle for biblical justice, who agonize over our responsibility for broken brothers and wasted sisters, the Eucharist should be the heart of our spirituality. But our Eucharist is a perilous experience. The peril is twofold, comes from two quarters. On the one hand, the Eucharist is the prime sacrament of unity, and yet it divides us. Not precisely the way it divided the early Corinthian community. But just as effectively: from the music to the ministers, from the exchange of peace to Communion in the hand, from the agenda and the baggage we bring with us. On the other hand, the Eucharist should propel our people to the poor of every dimension. Not only the suffering who share our faith; all those who are in pain. It should open our eyes as it does the eyes of Teresa: to see in every human the image of Christ, the Christ of Calvary—the real presence of Christ in those who labor and are heavy-burdened. But does it? How can it when only 30 percent of American Catholics are nourished by Christ's word and flesh at least twice a month? How can it when untold thousands who are so nourished close their ears when "the poor" are preached, when the very word "justice" conjures up lazy welfare folk living off our hard-earned money?

This is not a jeremiad against our people. The longer I live, the more convinced I am that "the buck stops...here." After God, the initiative rests with us. Paul was clear, unambiguous: "[God] has given us the ministry of reconciliation,...entrusting the ministry of reconciliation to us. So we are ambassadors for Christ, since God is making His appeal through us..." (2 Cor 5:18-20). Not indeed exclusively; baptism summons all Christians to be reconcilers. Still, in a sharp, singular way through our ordination. For ordination graces us powerfully to be leaders, to move the minds and hearts of men and women, to organize the charisms of our people so that each parish is a force for reconciliation—with God, with one another, with the earth.

How? Especially through the Eucharist. The Word of God and the flesh of Christ. Is there any power on earth more dynamic than these? Weak we may be, fearful, discouraged; but no weaker, no more fearful, no more discouraged than Paul. But, like Paul, "I can do all things through [the Lord] who strengthens me" (Phil 4:13). I can even preach with fire in my belly!

Yes, but only if I apply Paul to my own ministry: no love, no Eucharist.

San Alfonso House
Long Branch, New Jersey
September 12, 1994

16
TAKE CARE HOW YOU LISTEN
Twenty-fifth Week of the Year, Monday (A)

- Ezra 1:1-6
- Luke 8:16-18

Today's Gospel strikes me as splendidly pertinent for those who must preach God's word.[1] Why? Because it stresses *how:* how those whose task it is to be "light" to their world, to preach God's word, are expected to *listen* to God's word. You see, these three sentences are not isolated pieces. They take us back to earlier verses of Luke 8, the parable of the Sowed Seed and Jesus' explanation (Lk 8:4-15). So, let me (1) recall what the parable had to say; (2) suggest how, in light of the parable, we who must *preach* God's word have to *listen* to God's word; (3) end with a personal plea.

I

In Jesus' parable, there are four ways different people listen to the word coming from God.[2] First, there is the seed that falls "along the footpath" (v. 5). Here Jesus is speaking of those who hear the word of God but have no saving faith. To really hear God's word, I must react to it with faith. Many don't. Why not? Because the opportunity to do so "is snatched away, not by Jesus...but by evil personified, by the influence of what is opposed to the saving word itself."[3]

Second, there is the seed that falls "on rocky soil" (v. 6). Many there are who do react with faith, but it doesn't last; adversity breaks them, faith weakens, doesn't stand up under stress.

Third, there is the seed that falls "amid thornbushes" (v. 7). There are some who listen to the word of God, but it never matures in them; they "attain to no maturity in Christian life."[4] They are distracted—by anxieties, by riches, by pleasures, by all sorts of overpowering forces. The world is too much with them; listening never reaches a fruitful term.

Fourth, there is the seed that falls "into good ground" (v. 8). Here are believers who listen to the word of God with an open mind, an open heart, men and women who mature in their Christian living. Their great gift is persistence, perseverance; they never stop listening.

II

So much for the parable. This brings us to ourselves. The words of Jesus are supremely important for preachers, for those whose "light" God's people must be able to grasp: "Take care how you listen" (Lk 8:18). It's interesting, instructive, to see how Luke has modified Mark. Mark relates the same scene but has Jesus saying, "Pay attention to *what* you hear" (Mk 4:24). Luke stresses the *way* you listen rather than its object.

The how is so important. When I open the Scriptures to prepare a homily, I must indeed listen with a loving, saving faith; I must listen with an open mind and heart; I must listen with persistence and perseverance. But what does this mean more concretely? Several questions.

How aware am I that, in what I call "the Word of the Lord," God is speaking to me? Listening to Yahweh, listening to Jesus, is not the same as listening to a character out of a dead past. Listening to Scripture, within the liturgy or outside, is not the same as reading Augustine's *Confessions* or Gibran's *Prophet*, not the same as hearing a Shakespeare sonnet or Handel's *Messiah*. The Lord God, our Lord Christ, is speaking to me. Do I listen the way our Lady did, the mother who "kept all these things, pondering them in her heart" (Lk 2:19; see 2:51)? Do I listen as breathlessly as Moses listened to the Lord on Sinai? Do I marvel, like Jesus' townspeople, "at the words of grace" that fall from his lips (Lk 4:22)? When was the last time I exclaimed with the disciples returning from Emmaus, "Were not our hearts burning within us while [Jesus] was talking to us on the road, while he was opening the Scriptures to us?" (Lk 24:32). Do I say longingly and lovingly with Samuel of old, "Speak, Lord, for your servant is listening" (1 Sam 3:9, 10)? Or, do I really mean, as that delightful Princeton ethicist Paul Ramsey rephrased it, "Speak, Lord, and your servant will think it over"?

A small confession. For a number of years, especially in the 70s and 80s, I found the breviary b-o-r-i-n-g, especially the ceaseless repetition of the Psalms. Until.... Until I began to listen. Not to words alone, dreadfully familiar words: "O sing to the Lord a new song" (Ps 96:1); "Then they attached themselves to the Baal of Peor" (Ps 106:28); "Save me, O God, for the waters have come up to my neck" (Ps 69:1). I found myself listening to what the Lord might be saying to *me*, in *my* context, to *my* life: "Do not cast me off in the time of old age; do not forsake me when my strength is spent" (Ps 70:9). More recently, by listening like Mary and Samuel, with ears intent for every nuance, I discovered in the Psalms a God of justice:

> He delivers the needy when they call,
>> the poor and those who have no helper.
> He has pity on the weak and the needy,
>> and saves the lives of the needy.
> From oppression and violence He redeems their life,
>> and precious is their blood in His sight.
>
> (Ps 72:12-14)

The Psalms no longer induce sleep; the Psalms are for me God's constant cry to the unjust of every stripe, "Let my people go!"

This morning we learned from a master interpreter, John Donahue, the profound meaning of biblical justice; we discovered that justice is intrinsic to God's covenant with Israel and with the Church; we began to grasp the significance of Micah's declaration to the people of God's special choosing, "What does the Lord require of you but to do justice?" (Mic 6:8). Our fresh task through the days and years that lie ahead, a duty we dare not decline, is to make the biblical texts our own, plumb increasingly the unfathomable depths of God's just word, link God's word to the agonizing cry of the poor, the more effectively to preach the second great commandment of the law and the gospel, "You shall love your neighbor as yourself" (Mt 22:39). That commandment, Jesus said, "is like" the first: To love our sisters and brothers "is like" loving God.

Dare I conclude that *preaching* biblical justice, *preaching* the second great commandment of love, *my* preaching, "is like" loving God?

III

Finally, a personal plea. St. Jerome used to say that to be ignorant of Scripture is to be ignorant of Christ. I would add, to be ignorant of Scripture is to be ignorant of the *images* of Christ. I mean, our two Testaments provide divine ideas, in imaginatively human language, on the human family, on the People of God, on the Body of Christ, on the single community that was intended by a creating God, shattered by sin, re-created by Christ—the family that is now and always in danger of being dis-membered, fragmented, torn asunder.

The word of reconciliation is there, from imaginative Genesis to apocalyptic John. This is the word our people have to hear, are entitled to hear. But for *them* to listen, you and I have to preach God's word with understanding and love, with passion and compassion. To preach that way, we must really listen. Listen as we pray, listen as we meditate, listen as we proclaim. Listen with eagerness, with longing, at times in frustration, when all we can cry is "Please, Lord, open my ears!"

Yes, Lord, open not only my mouth but my ears. Before I open my mouth, grace me to listen to your voice—in the fierce raging of your prophets and the musical syllables of your psalmists, but especially in the Son who *is* your Word, spoken from eternity in your secret life, spoken in human syllables from Nazareth to Calvary, speaking to us now in the cry of the poor, the powerless. For only if I have listened dare I speak, dare I say "This is the word of the Lord."

San Damiano Retreat Center
Danville, California
September 20, 1993

17

HARSH TEACHING; WHO CAN LISTEN TO IT?
Twenty-sixth Sunday of the Year (B)

- Numbers 11:25-29
- James 5:1-6
- Mark 9:38-43, 45, 47-48

For the 30 percent of Catholics who worship regularly on Sunday, Rome has rolled out for your R&R a rough set of readings. On the face of it, three seemingly harsh reproofs. (1) If you're in the habit of tuning out TV's Protestant prophets, stow it! Moses tells you, "Would that all the Lord's people were prophets!" (Num 11:29). (2) If you are blessed with this world's goods, the Letter of James (actually a sermon) warns you: "Come now, you rich people, weep and wail for the miseries that are coming to you" (Jas 5:1). (3) Mark may well make you gasp, even perhaps recall gross memories, when his Jesus says: If any part of the body causes you to sin, cut it off, else you're in peril of hell. As his own disciples said when he promised his body to eat, "Harsh teaching; who can listen to it?" (Jn 6:60).

Now if *you* are puzzled, upset, embarrassed, what of your guest preacher? Shall I thrash you for watching "Chicago Hope"[1] instead of TV prophets? Or shall I lash out at you for not giving your surplus wealth to the Jesuits? Or shall I offer a laundry list of church scandals—in Rome, of course, not in Georgetown?

Actually, none of the above. And still, all three readings are too powerful, too challenging, too important for Christian living to be glossed over from ignorance or cowardice. Each has something quite positive to offer us—if we understand them aright. Not to turn a homily into a lecture; simply to suggest how even the most "offensive" passages in God's Book are still God's Word. And God's Word addressed not only to Israelites centuries ago, but to Christians trying to live that Word in confusing times. But they demand to be understood as God intended. So then, three passages, three points.

I

First, that puzzling word "prophecy." Is Moses serious? "Would that all the Lord's people were prophets"? Yes, if you understand that in the Hebrew Testament the prophet, in the first instance, was not someone who could predict the future, could tell you when the world would end, could foretell today whether baseball's owners and players will ever grow up.[2] The Hebrew prophets did make predictions, but even more importantly they were inspired by God to speak God's word in God's name,[3] or inspired by God to speak God's word in the name of the people.[4] Now to condemn the idolatry of priests and people; now to encourage the enslaved and the exiled; now to challenge Yahweh, "Thy will be changed."

What Moses was insisting on was a genuine peril at the time: putting all prophecy, all speaking in God's name, under institutional control.[5] No one dare speak in God's name unless he or she is officially designated to do so—and by a particular organization with exclusive rights so to designate.

This has troubled our own dear church down the ages. But for all the institutional control, unexpected prophets have sprung up like wildflowers. In the 14th century, Catherine of Siena, a woman, young, with no social position, "having cleared the nepotists and simonists out of Rome, rapped the knuckles of the pope in Avignon until he agreed to come back where he belonged."[6] Who today will dare say Luther was not speaking God's word when he castigated his church for the sordid sale of indulgences? I am convinced that Dorothy Day was speaking God's word when she reproved a New York cardinal for sending seminarians to replace striking gravediggers at a Catholic cemetery. The examples are endless, and regularly intriguing.

The problem this raises is a technical word: criteria. How can you tell whether someone is speaking God's word in God's name, speaking God's word in the name of the people? How can you tell whether God is speaking through Catherine of Siena or Martin Luther or Dorothy Day? Not always easy, I assure you. I myself find prophets most believable when they are transparently motivated by love—love even of the people they challenge. And humble enough to recognize that they just might be wrong.

The lesson for us today? A declaration of Vatican II that continues Moses' hope "Would that all God's people were prophets." I mean the council's statement, "The holy People of God shares...in Christ's prophetic office."[7] Each Christian has the obligation and the privilege of bearing witness to the gospel. By our lives, of course: by the way we put our faith into action, the way we parent, the way we do business, the way we react to the hungry and the thirsty, to the stranger and the homeless, to the sick and the imprisoned. But over and above that, "Would that every Christian spoke God's word—in the name of God or on behalf of the people." So-called prophets clog the airwaves, the Op-Ed page, our city streets. Hard to tell at times what God is saying, or even that it is God who is speaking. Why not you? Vatican II lauded your charismatic gifts, quoted Paul's first letter to the Christians of Corinth. For Paul insisted that the Spirit distributes among the faithful remarkable gifts for the common good: to utter wisdom, to utter knowledge, to prophesy...(1 Cor 12:7-11).

If a council and an apostle fail to grab you, listen to imaginative Jesuit William O'Malley:

> ...we can no longer depend on the comforting simplism of "The Church Teaching" and "The Church Taught"; there are too many Ph.D.'s out in the pews now. The magisterium and the People of God are now like Henry Higgins and Eliza Doolittle at the end of "Pygmalion." He had found a tatterdemalion flower girl and turned her into a lady. But once the metamorphosis took place, neither Higgins nor Eliza knew quite what to do about the new relationship. He was no longer the all-knowing teacher, and she no longer the biddable pupil. Not only does the official church have an obligation to listen more to the people, but the people have the intimidating obligation to speak up....[8]

So then, Elizas of the earth, speak up! You are not substitutes for a declining priesthood, to be relegated to the sidelines if and when we can buy more Roman collars. You share in Christ's prophetic office.

I only suggest that for today's prophet a touch of humor might help, for prophets from OT Jeremiah down to TV evangelists tend to be frighteningly grim. I recommend to you a banner I once saw at a women's liberation rally. It read, "Eve was framed."

II

Second, the troubling passage in the Letter of James. Especially the opening sentence, "You rich people, weep and wail for the miseries that are coming to you" (Jas 5:1). Out of context, it's a dread-full sentence; not only full of dread but open to misunderstanding. And yet the context is clear. This is not a denunciation of riches, of all the rich. The enemy is the unjust rich. Listen again: "The wages of the laborers who mowed your fields, which you kept back by fraud, cry out, and the cries of the harvesters have reached the ears of the Lord of hosts"

(v. 4). Even the harsh sentence, "You have murdered the just one, who does not resist you" (v. 6), may take us back to the Book of Sirach: "To take away a neighbor's living is to murder him; to deprive an employee of his wages is to shed blood" (Sir 34:22).

Harsh words, yes, but not unchristian. They remind me of so much I tend to forget. They remind me that money is powerful, for evil as well as for good. For good: Without money neither this lovely house of God nor Georgetown University would ever have been built. For evil: Remember the movie "Indecent Proposal"? Robert Redford buys from a husband a night of sex with his wife. The purchasing power? One million dollars. They remind me of the danger in two words, words St. Augustine termed "those ice-cold words 'mine and thine.'" I mean the danger in clinging possessively to anything or anyone, whether it's a Raggedy Ann doll or a person I delight in, my Jaguar or my Bible, an acre of land or a spot in the limelight. It's mine, I own it, and no one dare touch it. It reminds me that all I own I hold in stewardship for the Lord of all. Just because it is mine does not mean I can do with it as I will. My ideas are indeed mine, my strength, my brilliance, my money, all these the fruit of my industry, but only because the God of all gave me life to begin with, gave me what it takes to be the enviable person I have become. It reminds me of a profound thinker in the third century, Origen, who waxed passionate not against private property but to liberate the rich from the acquisitiveness, the greed, that the early Church regarded as a form of idolatry.

> God...knows that what a man loves with all his heart and soul and might—this for him is God. Let each one of us now examine himself and silently in his own heart decide which is the flame of love that chiefly and above all else is afire within him, which is the passion that he finds he cherishes more keenly than all others.... Whatever it is that weighs the heaviest in the balance of your affection, that for you is God.[9]

Worth scotch-taping to my refrigerator door: Whatever weighs heaviest in my affections, that for me is God.

III

Happily, that realization leads easily into our third problem, the command of Jesus: Whatever causes you to sin, cut it off. Now Jesus is not mandating mutilation. It's a typically Semitic way of speaking—graphic, vivid, even exaggerated. Like Jesus' condition for being his disciple: You have to "hate" father and mother, wife and children, sisters and brothers, even your own life. He whose whole life was love could not possibly be counseling genuine hatred. It's a striking Semitic way of getting a message across. The meaning is clear in Matthew: "Whoever loves father or mother, son or daughter more than me is not worthy of me" (Mt 10:37). Nothing, no one, comes before Christ.[10]

Similarly here. To fasten too firmly on the physical is to miss the point. The point? Whatever causes me to sin or leads others into sin, whatever supplants God in my life, get rid of it! This is basic to our Christian spirituality, for it echoes the first of the Ten Commandments in Exodus and Deuteronomy: "You shall have no other gods before me" (Exod 20:3; Deut 5:7).[11]

Terribly negative, you say? Possibly. And many a Catholic leaves that impression with our non-Catholic neighbors. Mass is an obligation, and the faith is an endless "don't"; Lent means "give up," and holiness says "cut it off." Tragic, for Christianity is not in the first instance negation, rejection, refusal, "cut it off." Christianity is the most powerful four-letter word humans have ever created: love. And that love touches simply everyone and everything. I am to love God with every fiber of my being. I am to love every man, woman, and child, whatever their color, however they smell, like another "I," as if I were standing in their shoes. And I am to care lovingly for the earth and all that lives and grows thereon, for the earth on which I dance so lightly, the earth I dare to rape and ravage, this earth keeps me alive. And I dare not forget the startling statement of St. Paul: This creation of God's love "waits with eager longing" to be "set free from its bondage to decay," to "obtain the freedom of the glory of the children of God" (Rom 8:19-22). Somehow, in God's mysterious design, the earth is to share in my salvation, in my redemption.

No, "cut it off" is not mutilation; it is liberation. It frees me to love without reservation, not trapped in the self-love where everything— things, people, even God—revolves around me. There is a fascinating paradox here: The more I focus on the God who lives in me, on the people God cherishes in a special way because they are more needy, and on the earth that God once saw "was very good" (Gen 1:31), the richer will be my delight in myself. It makes sense. For human living is a matter of relationships: with God, with people, with earth. Love God, love people, love earth, and "cutting it off" takes care of itself.

My joy today lies in this: I find all this in you. For this I shall be for ever grateful. Literally...for ever.

Holy Trinity Church
Washington, D.C.
September 25, 1994

18

NOT BECAUSE *THEY* ARE CATHOLIC....
Twenty-seventh Week of the Year, Monday (B)

- Galatians 1:1-6
- Luke 10:25-37

Quite some years ago, I was privileged to address the annual Conference of Ohio Pastors. I cannot remember what *I* said, but I cannot forget what a black pastor from Texas said. He was discoursing—actually he was preaching—on the parable of the Good Samaritan. I mean the man who was traveling from Jerusalem to Jericho, fell among robbers, was beaten half to death, was left to die. I mean the man who lay helpless at the side of the road while a Jewish priest "saw him [and] passed by on the other side" (Lk 10:31). I mean the despised Samaritan who "was moved with compassion" and "showed him mercy" (vv. 33, 37).

One powerful phrase in that sermon I have never forgotten. The priest—the pastor explained in a quiet but passionate rumble—could handle anything that had to do with the temple in Jerusalem: the vestments, the showbread, the Torah, the ark of the covenant. What he could not handle was "the évent on the Jericho road."

"The évent on the Jericho road." That phrase echoed and re-echoed throughout the sermon. Not only that. It has rumbled in my consciousness ever since. This evening I commend it to you for the life of justice that beckons you and me.[1] Let's look at our Jericho, first the half-dead, then those who can inject new life.

I

First, the half-dead. You see, the Jericho road is your road and mine. For where most of us live, the men and women shaped by God for the freedom of God's children have in a genuine sense fallen among robbers. Priests in urban ministry across the country experience this, experience human and inhuman living that is at times harrowing, leaves men, women, and children feeling only half alive. What do these priests tell us?

They tell us that these good people are ceaselessly struggling to simply survive. Millions have experienced, often still experience, what it means to do without: without food, without education, without work, without money, without the good things of God's earth you and I take for granted.

Priests in urban ministry tell us that, for these people, the family is not our current father, mother, child and a half. It is the extended family. There may be 13 or 16 in a single home—brothers, sisters, babies born out of wedlock, a grandmother at 40 parenting small children. The advantage? A New Testament bonding, recognition that everyone is a brother or sister. Disadvantage? It doesn't always work. Crack and coke, guns, AIDS, prison—a dis-ease that destroys relationships.

Priests in urban ministry speak of nihilism—a pervasive feeling that there is no future beyond this desperate moment, settling a score, proving yourself a man. And so you have kids killing kids, a life for a Reebok, a poverty that causes personal depression. Expensive clothes, rap music, the stress is on today; life is for now. In my D.C. backyard youngsters are preparing their own funerals—where to be waked, how to be dressed, how to look. For their experience—over 200 of their playmates killed by gunfire—tells them they cannot expect to be around very long.

On the other hand, there is something heartening here, reasons for hoping. (1) Their struggle puts many of them, perhaps most of them, into the camp of the Hebrew Testament *anawim*. I mean those pious, humble folk, originally the materially poor, oppressed, downtrodden, who were so conscious of their spiritual need, so aware of their dependence, that they looked to the Lord for strength and help, looked to God as their Savior. (2) There is an openness to rescue, to the power of God. Ever so many believe that "Someone bigger than me" has to come and straighten things out. (3) There is a sense of healing. Not so much from doctors and priests. Rather the expectation that God will bring healing, that God cares, God heals (even if God doesn't always cure); somehow God will make it come right.

II

Now for those who can inject new life. In one sense, it's a gleeful Gospel for the laity. The priest sees the victim; indeed he does. What does he do? What so many of us do today: He "passed by on the other side" (v. 31). So too the levite. Who does biblical justice? Who is faithful to a responsibility that stems from his faith in Yahweh, his faith in Moses, his faith in the Holy Law? A Samaritan.[2] A member of a religious group of whom the evangelist John noted, "Jews, remember, use nothing in common with Samaritans" (Jn 4:9). And still, this Samaritan, disdained by Jews, did not check his victim out, did not ask, "Are you a Samaritan or a Jew?" He simply took seriously the command of God he reverenced in Leviticus, "You shall love your neighbor as yourself" (Lev 19:18). And because he did so love, dying gave rise to new life.

A fascinating parable, especially for men and women concerned for biblical justice, struggling to be faithful to relationships, to responsibilities that stem from a covenant. Remember the lawyer's question, "Who is my neighbor?" (Lk 10:29). After the parable, Jesus does not address himself directly to that question. He turns the question on its head. Not "Your neighbor is so-and-so, the man who fell among robbers," but "Which of these three, do you think, was a neighbor to the man who fell into the hands of the robbers?" (v. 36). Don't ask who belongs to God's people, who therefore can be a worthy recipient of my neighborly attention. Ask rather how a member of God's chosen people must act when someone is in distress—anyone, whatever that person's ethnic or religious group. Because he does what the law commands, this pariah, this schismatic, this "outcast Samaritan shows that he is a neighbor, a member of God's people, one who inherits eternal life."[3]

Interesting, isn't it? It was not in their love of *God* that the priest and the levite were lacking; their dedicated life attests to that. Where they were found wanting was in the second great commandment of the law and the gospel.

It reminds me once again of a true story told by John Carr of the United States Catholic Conference's Department of Social Justice and World Peace. Not long ago, at a gathering of Catholics concerned for social justice, one of the participants, a gentleman gifted with years of Catholic education, asked the speaker: "Why do we try to help all these people? We never ask them what exactly they believe, whether they go to church, or even whether they are Catholic." The speaker responded: "We don't do this because *they* are Catholic; we do it because *we* are Catholic." The speaker? A cardinal: James Aloysius Hickey of Washington D.C. Like Jesus, he too turned the question on its head.

An intriguing, perhaps troubling meditation for this week. Not "Who counts as my neighbor?" Rather "What sort of neighbor am I?"

What kind of priest? How Christian? How human? For the command "Go and do likewise" (v. 37) was hardly addressed to an isolated Jewish lawyer. It rings imperiously down the ages.

Concretely, how do I handle "the event on *my* Jericho road"?

Marie Joseph Spiritual Center
Biddeford, Maine
October 3, 1994

19
THERE IS A CHURCH,
ALIVE AND PROSPEROUS....
Twenty-eighth Week of the Year, Monday (A)

- Romans 1:1-7
- Luke 11:29-32

A recent issue of the *National Catholic Reporter* carried a short, pungent article by a professor at the University of Tulsa. A prolific writer, usually coauthoring with his wife Denise, John Carmody has been struggling courageously with a life-threatening malignancy. His article "took off" from a liturgy in his parish church: everything "formal and formulaic," all "namby-pamby, bourgeois, tame," a sermon read tonelessly, without the glow of the Good News. John asserted passionately:

> There is a church, alive and prosperous, wherever two things come together: people's most pressing concerns and Jesus the Christ. When these two things do not come together, there is no church alive and prosperous. There is no worship worthy of the name, no imperative to preach Good News to the poor, to cure the blind and lame, to make justice roll down like a mighty torrent.[1]

In that context, with the liturgical readings in mind, let me speak to the problem that some wag has called "the bored again Catholic." Concretely, let me focus (1) on Paul, (2) on Jesus, (3) on you and me.[2]

I

First, St. Paul, specifically the opening lines of his letter to the Christians of Rome. Picture this fellow. He *may* have been short and bald, beard thick and nose unmistakable, eyebrows touching, legs bowed;[3] and still, impressive, forceful, fiery. Paul himself was aware what some were saying of him: "His letters are weighty and strong, but his bodily presence is weak, and his speech contemptible" (2 Cor 10:10). He is not one of the Twelve, yet he calls himself an apostle, "sent neither by human commission nor from human authorities, but through Jesus Christ and God the Father" (Gal 1:1). He calls himself "a slave of Jesus Christ" (Rom 1:1). Not only because every Christian should be a servant of Christ; more immediately because he is a preacher of the gospel serving the Christian community.[4]

The pregnant point is, Paul is obsessed by two realities, the same two John Carmody found woefully lacking in the parish homily. I mean ...Christ and people. The key to his theology, to his understanding of God's new mode of salvation, is passionately proclaimed in his first letter to the Christians of Corinth, two powerful sentences we repeat so often that they are in peril of turning stale, tasteless, lifeless. Etch them on your hearts: "It pleased God, through the foolishness of what we preach, to save those who believe. For Jews demand signs [miracles] and Greeks seek wisdom [a religious system], but we proclaim Christ crucified, a stumbling block to Jews and foolishness to Gentiles, but to those who are the called [who have accepted the gospel], both Jews and Greeks, Christ the power of God and the wisdom of God" (1 Cor 1:21-24). At the center of Paul's soteriology is what he calls so simply "the story of the cross" (v. 18).

But Paul is not concerned to explain what we theologians used to call the ontological constitution of Christ, what Christ is in his inmost being, Christ "in se." His Christology is functional; it serves a purpose— a people purpose. He preaches "Christ crucified," Christ central to human living, Christ for us. "You are God's children," he tells the Corinthians, "through your union with Christ Jesus, who became *for us* wisdom from God, our uprightness, our sanctification, our redemption" (v. 30).[5] For Paul the gospel is not an abstraction; it is "the power of God for salvation" (Rom 1:16). It is *dynamis*, dynamite, for every human person born into this world.

II

Let's move from Paul to Jesus. Today's Gospel contains more than meets the naked eye. Here too there is question of Jesus and people. Jonah, Luke's Jesus tells us, "became a sign to the people of Nineveh" (Lk 11:30). How? Not by the miracle of his deliverance from the belly of the great fish. By the power of his preaching, the power of God's word in Jonah's words, the prophet's powerful call to repentance. Mass conversion of the Ninevites: "The people of Nineveh believed God; they proclaimed a fast, and everyone, great and small, put on sackcloth" (Jonah 3:5). Even the king "rose from his throne, removed his robe, covered himself with sackcloth, and sat in ashes" (v. 6). And Jesus goes on to say: "[The Ninevites] repented at the proclamation of Jonah, and see, something greater than Jonah is here!" (Lk 11:32). In fact, Jesus' wisdom exceeds the wisdom of fabled Solomon.

But neither Luke nor Jesus is interested in abstract wisdom. For Luke, the important thing is hearing God's word proclaimed by Jesus and keeping it. Listen to the verse immediately preceding our passage: "Blessed are those who listen to the word of God and observe it" (Lk 11:28). "Luke holds up for imitation by his Gentile readers and all disciples the generous response given to God's word by nonelect people,"[6] by the people of Nineveh and the queen of Sheba. Jesus' countrymen "kept demanding from him a sign from heaven" (Lk 11:16), some "flamboyant portent" they could see or hear that would establish his authority, make him credible.[7] They failed to recognize the only sign that would be given: the heaven-sent wisdom Jesus came to preach.

What we do not hear in today's liturgy is what Jesus goes on to declare. His disciples, specifically those who preach Jesus as the light, must allow that light to shine in the darkness, to shine for men and women who are struggling for a way to come in out of the darkness (vv. 33-36).

III

This leads directly into my third point: the significance of the biblical passage for you and me. Let me take you back to 1975, to a quite remarkable papal document, Paul VI's apostolic exhortation *Evangelii nuntiandi*, usually known as *Evangelization in the Modern World*.[8] Pope Paul made it pellucidly clear that to evangelize involves two indispensable facets: Jesus and people.

First, Jesus. "There is no authentic evangelization unless the name and teaching, the life and promises, the kingdom and mystery of Jesus the Nazarene, Son of God, are preached."[9] To evangelize is to proclaim "that in Jesus Christ, the Son of God who became man, died and rose from the dead, salvation is offered to every man [and woman] as a gracious gift inspired by God's mercy."[10]

True, beyond debate. But equally clear is the pope's insistence that to evangelize is not simply to proclaim Christ. Evangelization, Paul insisted, "must be a message, especially strong and pointed today, of liberation."[11] Liberation from what? From "hunger, chronic illnesses, illiteracy, penury, injustice at the international level and especially in

commercial relations, and economic and cultural neocolonialism...."[12]
A little later: "The Church certainly considers it highly important to
establish structures which are more human, more just, more respectful
of the rights of the person, less oppressive and coercive."[13] Not sheerly
secular activity. Here is a vision of gospel liberation that is splendidly
balanced. Listen to Paul VI:

> ... in proclaiming liberation and ranging herself with all who toil
> and suffer for it, the Church cannot allow herself or her mission to
> be limited to the purely religious sphere while she ignores the
> temporal problems of [the human person]. At the same time,
> however, she affirms the primacy of her spiritual role, refuses to
> replace the proclamation of God's reign with the preaching of
> various purely human liberations, and insists that even her
> contribution to liberation is incomplete and imperfect if she fails
> to preach salvation in Jesus Christ.[14]

It is precisely here that you and I are addressed. For, as Paul VI
declared, "even the most perfect structures and the most ideal systems
quickly become inhuman unless the inhuman bent of [the human]
heart is corrected, unless those who live in or control these structures
are converted in heart and mind."[15] How will conversion come if you
and I do not preach it, if you and I only *preach* it but do not live it? Not a
once-for-all event; a fresh turning to Christ each day, an ever more total
self-giving to all the people we are privileged to serve. *All* our people;
for all of them, like all of us, are "poor," not sufficiently selfless,
insufficiently responsive to the graces God ceaselessly holds out, hardly
as "perfect as [our] heavenly Father is perfect" (Mt 5:48), so often
reluctant to love our sisters and brothers as Jesus has loved us.

Let me close where I began, with my good friend John Carmody.
He went on to say: "Ah, God: If you are boring, we have missed you.
Nothing is so real as you, nothing so living.... Gathering in [Jesus']
name, speaking the truth about what throbs in our hearts and shapes
our world, we can be his proper church, his own people, real at last—
human beings."[16]

Jesuit Center for Spiritual Growth
Wernersville, Pennsylvania
October 11, 1993

20
WHOEVER WELCOMES ONE SUCH CHILD....
Twenty-ninth Sunday of the Year (B)

- Isaiah 53:10-11
- Hebrews 4:14-16
- Mark 10:35-45

Today's Gospel scene is packed with insights. Insights into what it means to be a Christian. Specifically, what it means to be a Christian leader. James and John, who should have known better, are startlingly blunt with Jesus: "We want you to do for us whatever we ask of you" (Mk 10:35). And what is it they want? Status in the kingdom to come. "When you, Jesus, preside at the messianic banquet at the end of time, we want to sit at your right and at your left; we want the seats of power, where people will wait on us, serve us, bow before us." Jesus' response? "Can you suffer and die as I shall?" Their confident answer: "Why, of course we can." Then comes the lesson in leadership. "Yes, you will suffer and die as I do; but seats of power? What earthly rulers and lords, despots and tyrants have? This is not for you. Why not? Because it is not for me. I took your flesh not to be served but to serve, to die for others. If you want to be great in my kingdom, if you want to be first where I reign, you become a slave of everyone." Notice the Greek word: not just a servant; a slave. Total self-giving.

It is in this context that on this Sunday we focus on children. For as we search the signs of our times, as we struggle to understand what this moment in history demands of us, as we seek to discover urgent Christian service, as we ask of Jesus not what he can do for us but what we can do for him, the most vulnerable of humans loom before us. So then, three stages to today's homily: (1) today's child; (2) today's Christian; (3) today's service.

I

First, today's child. Look at our own dear "land of the free." An America where the infant mortality rate is higher than that of 19 other industrialized nations. An America where in 1990, in one year alone, 407,000 minors were placed in foster homes. An America where each day at least three children die of injuries inflicted by abusive parents. An America where each day over 500 children 10 to 14 begin using illegal drugs, over a thousand start on alcohol. An America where one child in eight has an alcoholic parent. An America where each day over 1400 teenage girls become mothers—two thirds of them unmarried. An America where among teens 15 to 19 the third-leading cause of death is firearms. An America whose capital city starts school with a weapons check. An America where the rate of teenage suicide has tripled in 30 years, where a million youngsters sleep on our streets each night. An America where HIV infection is a national disaster. An America where each year 1.6 million children are forcibly prevented from ever seeing the light of day. An America where there are greater tax benefits for breeding horses than for raising children. An America where one of every four youngsters you see is living in some sort of hell.

I look at my own back yard. In the District of Columbia a dismaying trend has recently come to light. Children in Washington are planning their own funerals: how they want to look, how be dressed, where be waked. Not out of curiosity, playacting; not from a Christian consciousness of death's significance. They simply do not believe they will be around very long, have every reason to suspect they will not grow up. Where they play, coke and crack are homicidal kings. In a five-year period, 224 of their childhood friends died from gunfire. Some were deliberate targets, others just bystanders, at least one lying in a cradle. And so the living little ones have begun planning for the worst, as if their own murders are inevitable, as if their own dreams will surely be just as cruelly cut short. Children....

Now cast your eyes across the world. Do you know how many children may well die this decade alone, the 90s, most from diseases we have learned to cure? One hundred and fifty million.

II

Second, what is a Christian reaction to all this? Sympathy? Tears? Get that bloated stomach off my TV? Things are tough all over? Pope John Paul II phrased it bluntly: "In the Christian view, our treatment of children becomes a measure of our fidelity to the Lord himself,"[1] the Lord who asserted, "Whoever welcomes one such child in my name welcomes me" (Mt 18:5). Today's Christian must echo the United Nations Children's Fund that phrased the pertinent moral principle in 1990 with devastating clarity:

...whether a child survives or not, whether a child is well-nourished or not, whether a child is immunized or not, whether a child has a school to go to or not, should not have to depend on whether interest rates rise or fall, on whether commodity prices go up or down, on whether a particular political party is in power, on whether the economy has been well managed or not, on whether a country is at war or not, or on any other trough or crest in the endless and inevitable undulations [of] political and economic life in the modern nation state.[2]

But we echo UNICEF not primarily because we share its milk of human kindness, its admirable awareness that the world's treatment of children is ethically unjust. Indeed it is. We are not simply giving to children what they have a right to expect, a right that can be proven from philosophy and has often been written into law. Good as such motivation is, the Christian approach rises above the sheerly ethical. Our motivation is biblical justice.

And what is biblical justice? Fidelity to relationships, to responsibilities, especially as these stem from our covenant with God in Christ. What relationships, what responsibilities? To God, whom we simply must love above all else, with all our mind and heart and soul and strength. To every brother and sister shaped in God's own image, loving them not merely as much or as little as we love ourselves, but as if we were standing in their shoes. To the very earth on which we dance so lightly, the earth that nourishes us with its life, the earth we ravage and rape as if we owned it, as if there is to be no tomorrow.

In our relationships with sisters and brothers, a preferential option must go to the poor. Not because they are better or holier than the well-to-do, but because they are in greater need. This is the way our God comes through to us in the pages of God's own Book. This is what the God of the Prior Testament demanded of the kings that served God's people. And the "poor" are not only those who are economically disadvantaged. The poor are all those who weep and bleed under oppression. The poor are those of whom Yahweh spoke through the prophet Isaiah (Isa 58:6-7):

> Is not this the fast that I choose:
>   to loose the bonds of injustice,
>   to undo the thongs of the yoke?
> Is it not to share your bread with the hungry,
>   and bring the homeless poor into your house;
> when you see the naked, to cover them,
>   and not to hide yourself from your own kin?

The poor are those of whom Jesus spoke when he told us on what basis we will ultimately be judged: "I was hungry and you gave me food, I was thirsty and you gave me something to drink, I was a stranger and you welcomed me, I was naked and you gave me clothing, I was sick and you took care of me, I was in prison and you visited me" (Mt 25:35-36). In Christian service it is Christ whom we serve in his images.

III

These principles that undergird all Christian service lead into my third point: today's service. If it is the greater need that summons us more urgently, then our children, the most vulnerable, the most defenseless, of our sisters and brothers, have a special claim on our service. But what sort of service? Concretely, what are we to do?

Actually, no homilist can spell out what any given Christian must do. All of us must ask with Saul hurled from his horse, "What am I to do, Lord?" (Acts 22:10). So much depends on who I am, where I am, the gifts with which God has graced me. But this much can be said: We need not fly to Bosnia or the sub-Sahara to find that there is "no room in the inn" for the world's children. Our "inns" stare us in the face. Some suggestions may prove practical.

First, the children within our own families. It is not only the physically and sexually abused that cry out to us. All our children do: cry loudly or mutely for attention, for love, for good example, for parents who live their baptism, their consecration to Christ, who have not been caught up in the rugged individualism that has captured our culture, the race that is to the swift, the shrewd, the savage. Are our children, for all practical purposes, latchkey children—children who rarely see their parents, spend more time with TV than with mother and father? Early Christians called the family a small church, a domestic church. It should be the Church in miniature, a community of love. Is mine?

Second, what are the children's issues within my parish limits? Where do they hurt? Hunger? One-parent families? Inferior education? Drug dealers on the streets? Violence against or among children? Not only the Catholic children; all children. I believe it was James Cardinal Hickey of Washington D.C. who was asked by a devout Catholic why we help so many people who are not Catholic, and replied, "We don't help them because *they* are Catholic but because *we* are Catholic." Is there anything I do within the parish? Am I personally active? Do I visit the children's wards in hospitals, homes for the orphaned? Am I involved in the schools? Does my parish have special events, social and liturgical, for children, for youth? Do I ever look into the vacant, hopeless eyes of a child unloved?

Third, beyond the parish boundaries: community outreach. The day of the Lone Ranger is gone. To get things done on a large scale, we have to organize, become part of something larger, more influential than the individual. Am I involved in any civic organizations that focus on children? Have I ever written to my representatives in Congress on children's issues, complimented them, challenged them? Do I support Bread for the World, Covenant House, the Children's Defense Fund? Am I even aware of the remarkable work they do? What do I know about the bishops' long-term campaign Putting Children and Families First?

I too have a dream. A dream that would transfigure the face of America. I dream that between now and the birthday of the Christ Child each Christian will look into the eyes of one child, a single child abused or neglected, homeless or hungry, unloved or unwanted, be moved to anguish at the experience, and resolve to change that child's life, give him or her a tiny but real hope that tomorrow will be different, worth living for, worth waiting for. One child. But in that one child...always the Christ Child.

Our Lady of Mercy Church
Potomac, Maryland
October 16, 1994

21
DON'T YOU HAVE SOMEONE YOU'D DIE FOR?
Thirtieth Week of the Year, Monday (A)

- Romans 8:12-17
- Luke 13:10-17

Last week, *Time* magazine's cover story dealt with "Rock's Anxious Rebels."[1] The rebels are angry young rockers who give voice to the passions and fears of a generation. They cover ear-catching categories: Glam Rock and Hard Rock, Party Animals and Teenage Wasteland, Punk and Funk, Acid Rock and Perky Pop, Hippies and Heavy Messengers, Tunesmiths and Arena Fillers. Slam them, if you will, on all sorts of justifiable issues; blast Funk's Porno for Pyros; rage against "alternative rock" for its focus on despair, lust, and confusion. What impresses me is the passion in their guts, their ability to fire up thousands of listeners, turn on millions of purchasers, send shivers up human spines, express the hates and loves, the hopes and fears, of a whole generation. When Tanya Donnelly sings "Don't you have someone you'd die for?", she can shake your soul.

Increasingly, what touches me in Jesus is his gift for moving people, generating excitement, turning listeners on. Not indeed by music, not with heavy metal and bouncy tunes. How does he do it? Let's (1) tune in on today's Gospel, (2) reflect on Jesus' secret, and (3) turn the light of that secret on ourselves and our apostolate.[2]

I

We are dealing with a liberating action of Jesus on the Sabbath. Luke has six stories that narrate such actions on that holy day. He announces as his mission release to captives and freedom for the oppressed (Lk 4:16-30). He heals a man with demon sickness (4:31-37). He defends his disciples plucking and eating heads of grain (6:1-5). He cures a withered hand (6:6-11), a man with dropsy (14:1-6), and here, today, a woman bent double. All on the Sabbath.

Take a closer look at the woman "unable to fully straighten herself" (Lk 13:11). See how Jesus operates. First, he calls her over to him. She has made no appeal to him, has not asked to be healed. Second, he simply says, "Woman, you are set free of your infirmity" (v. 12). Third, he lays his hands on her. Instantly she straightens and keeps glorifying God.

It's the personal touch, the way Jesus dealt with all humans—men and women, children too. You remember the hemorrhaging woman who simply touched the hem of his cloak; how, surrounded by a massive crowd, he searched her out, looked all around for her, wanted to look into her eyes. With sensitive, healing hands he touches lepers, Peter's mother-in-law, the eyes of two blind men, a deaf man's tongue, the coffin of a mother's only son, little children, the ear severed by one of his disciples. For this is the flesh he took to save. He does not shrink from it, from its aging and its wrinkling, its sores and its scars, its weakness and its vulnerability. He does not focus on "the bold and the beautiful,"[3] on the high and mighty.

Why? Because no one is excluded from salvation. Especially those who were not esteemed in Palestinian society, or at least in the experience of Luke: Samaritans and sinners, women and toll collectors, criminals and the poverty-stricken. Let's call them, in biblical language, "the poor." Not only is no one excluded; the whole person is to be healed, is to be saved—body as well as soul. For, as Jean Mouroux once expressed it, a separated soul, whether in heaven or hell, yearns for its body with a purely natural impulse of love.

More than that. Jesus heals indiscriminately on any day of the week. The sacredness of the Sabbath is no reason to cease healing. Compassion is not constricted by the day of the week. In fact, the Sabbath is sacralized, made sacred, by healing. "This woman is a daughter of Abraham, and Satan has kept her tied up [like an animal tethered to a trough[4]] for 18 long years. Did she not have to be set free from this bondage on the day of Sabbath?" (Lk 13:16). On his journey up to Jerusalem, his journey to the city of his destiny, "where he will meet evil in another form in his own life,"[5] Jesus makes clear that human needs, the needs of men and women, take precedence over religious obligations, even such basic obligations as observance of the Sabbath.

II

What does all this suggest about Jesus' secret, the secret of his effect on men and women: on farmers and fisherfolk, on toll collectors and taxpayers, on Martha and Mary and the woman taken in adultery, on a Roman centurion and a Pharisee named Nicodemus? Two facets strike me quickly.

First and obviously, the personal touch. You know, the Son of God did not have to take our flesh as his own. And when he did, any single action (his fasting in the wilderness), any single gesture (feeding the 5000), any single word of Jesus ("Father, forgive them") could have worked our salvation. Why, then, the torturous journey from Bethlehem through Nazareth to Jerusalem? Because the Lord loved us sinful folk, all of us, so incredibly that he wanted to share our experience of human and inhuman living. Not only know it intellectually, with a divine mind that encompassed all that might ever happen. Rather, live it with us, from Mary of Nazareth's womb to Joseph of Arimathea's tomb. The weariness and the sweat, the insults and the stones, betrayal with a friend's kiss and crucifixion among his own people. Yes, he had someone he'd die for: every single one of us. Not a misty mass called humanity; each one of us as a unique person.

A second facet: within Jesus' love for all of us, a special love for "the poor." Not simply the poverty-stricken. Jesus' poor are the disadvantaged, the disabled, the powerless, all those crucified between heaven and earth, unable to see God through the clouds, their dear ones through tears. Why these? Because these need him all the more— more than the advantaged, the able, the powerful.

Not that Jesus disdained the privileged. All of us need him, all humans; for, as Jesus declared solemnly, "Without me you can do nothing" (Jn 15:5). Nothing that moves us a single positive step towards God, towards our salvation.

III

Finally, let's turn the light of Jesus' secret on ourselves and our apostolate—specifically, preaching the just word. Obstacles obstruct us, as they obstructed Jesus. Many committed Catholics close their ears to us because they see us occupying turf where we have no right to be. Others, like a prominent bishop in California, tell me frankly that "there are more important issues than social justice." A fair number of women will not listen to our preaching on justice because to them an exclusively male priesthood is a striking symbol of injustice. It can be dismaying, discouraging. How to respond? The way Jesus did.

First, the personal touch, the touch of genuine love. I am reminded of one of St. Augustine's remarkable insights: "There is nothing that invites love more than to be beforehand in loving; and that heart is overhard which, even though it were unwilling to bestow love, would be unwilling to return it."[6] Not simply loving thoughts, love at a distance. Healing words; at times healing hands. Ever in the mold of Jesus, with the mind of Jesus. Softening hard hearts with the gentleness of Jesus; changing cemented minds with the persuasion of Jesus; firing cold souls with the passion of Jesus. For that, you and I must have "fire in the belly." For only fire will strike fresh sparks—the fire of a love that never despairs, never gives up, even when the cost is crucifixion. For we dare not forget the paradox that founds our Christian hope: Life comes through death. Not only the dying of God-in-flesh; our own dying, particularly to our best-laid plans for the coming of the kingdom.

Second, a special love for the disadvantaged, all those who experience more of Christ's crucifixion than of his resurrection. Many of us have lost, or have never had, the sensitivity to evil that marked the Hebrew prophets—men like Isaiah and Jeremiah, Amos and Micah. Some surely share that sensitivity; but it is usually those who have experienced firsthand the sorry existence of the poor and the imprisoned, the hungry and the downtrodden. More of us simply deplore injustice; we are against sin; we take up collections for the homeless Somali. Somehow our people should sense that we feel fiercely, that, as Vatican II put it, we share in "the joys and the hopes, the griefs and the anxieties of the people of this age, especially those who are poor or in any way afflicted."[7]

Let me close with a thought that intrigues me. Should not *our* Sabbath be each week a graced opportunity to heal so many who are "unable to fully straighten" themselves? Bodies maybe; spirits surely. How? By words. Not naked syllables. Words ablaze with the flame of the Spirit, issuing from a mouth touched, as Jeremiah's was, by the hand of the Lord, lips burning with God's hot coals. You see, it is not only to Jeremiah that the Lord says, "Now I have put my words in your mouth" (Jer 1:9). My words...in your mouth.

Lumen Christi Retreat House
Schriever, Louisiana
October 25, 1993

22
IF YOU HAD FAITH....
Thirty-second Week of the Year, Monday (A)

- Wisdom 1:1-7
- Luke 17:1-6

> Then the apostles said to the Lord, "Increase our faith!" But the Lord said: "If you had faith the size of a mustard seed, you would say to this mulberry seed, 'Be uprooted and planted in the sea,' and it would obey you" (Lk 17:6).

In the context of that astounding passage, allow me to move faith in three directions: (1) to a hospital in Washington, D.C.; (2) to a small country called Palestine; (3) to a beloved diocese called Winona.

I

First, a hospital in Washington, D.C. It was eight years ago. I was visiting an ailing but mobile friend in George Washington Hospital. Before I left, she took me down the hall to another room. On one of the beds lay a black lady somewhere in her seventies. On her face, all through my visit, was a radiant smile of genuine joy; her strikingly blue eyes seemed to sparkle. She spoke of God as of someone closer to her bedside than I was, spoke of current events as if she were right there in the midst of them.

Since age 13, I learned, she had spent much of her life as a live-in servant. Against all the odds, she mentioned two little boys, blood brothers, she had helped bring up in Baltimore a half century ago. She related how she used to scrub the face of the younger boy, Francis, saying the while: "Tad looks good with a dirty face, but you don't." The two lads, she said, grew up to be priests, Jesuit priests; and to her delight I realized, and told her, that I had taught both of them in the seminary at Woodstock.

This is not a commercial for vocations. That bedridden black lady, merry in God, in love with God, aglow with life, was totally blind, and both her legs had been amputated. When I left her, I blessed her; but I knew that in reality she had blessed me. And ever since that evening, all these latter days when I've been wrestling with Luke on a faith that can move mountains and mulberry trees, Mary Evans has haunted me. She has ripped faith out of abstractions, out of outer space, brought it down to a grim earth, made me look at it through her sightless eyes, walk it on her helpless stumps.

That blind, legless lady moved more than mountains and trees; she moved human hearts, made humans like me want to be better than we were. Under God, she increased my faith.

II

To see where such faith comes from, Mary Evans' and mine, let's fly to Palestine. Palestine when the Son of God walked this earth in our flesh. I suggest that, if you are searching for a penetrating summation of gospel faith, you mull over Luke's parable of the Sower. How does Jesus describe his disciples? "Those who listen to [God's] word and hold on to it with a noble and generous mind" (Lk 8:15). Paul fills that out with a remarkable word: Faith is "obedience" (Rom 1:5; 16:26), a submission, a personal commitment to God. It is a complete surrender to a revealing Lord.

This is not just a question of definitions. What is amazing in Gospel faith is that Jesus himself lived by faith and died with faith. I know, this is not the prevailing medieval tradition, but the best of today's theologians, scholars as different from each other as Rahner and Balthasar, find in faith a significant segment of the self-emptying that is the Incarnation: Jesus experiencing our human condition of ignorance and darkness. It is only faith that makes sense of the agony in the garden and the apparent abandonment on the cross. That is why Balthasar can argue that

> Jesus is the perfect fulfillment of the OT understanding of faith: through his obedience, his surrender to his Father, his perseverance in times of trial, he fulfills the OT covenant, and as the Letter to the Hebrews (12:2) says, becomes the pioneer and perfecter of our faith.[1]

Very much like us, Jesus died not with experience of resurrection; he died with faith in his Father, with hope of life for ever. Here Rahner is incredibly insightful, terribly moving:

According to Scripture we may safely say that Jesus in his life was the *believer*.... In the unity of faith, hope, and love, Jesus surrendered himself in his death unconditionally to the absolute mystery that he called his Father, into whose hands he committed his existence, when in the night of his death and God-forsakenness he was deprived of everything that is otherwise regarded as the content of a human existence.... Everything fell away from him, even the perceptible security of the closeness of God's love, and in this trackless dark there prevailed silently only the mystery...to which he calmly surrendered himself as to eternal love and not to the hell of futility.... He who came out of God's glory did not merely descend into our human life, but also fell into the abyss of our death, and his dying began when he began to live and came to an end on the cross when he bowed his head and died.[2]

III

Mary Evans and Jesus of Nazareth compel my third point: Winona.[3] Not that I know the priests of Winona more than superficially. But I am concerned, obsessed if you will, by a paradox, an apparent contradiction, in the American Catholic priesthood. The Second Vatican Council listed proclamation of the gospel as a priest's "primary duty."[4] And yet, across our nation our people on the whole expect little or nothing when we mount the pulpit, rarely look for their faith to be deepened or expanded, do not anticipate any kind of conversion. As the Catholic president of the University of Rochester summed it up, "Saturday Night Live, Sunday morning deadly."

The solution? No single suggestion can turn the tide. But in the light of today's Gospel, I insist that if liturgical preaching is to contribute to a congregation's growth in faith, eloquence is not enough. I must come through to my people, to the faithful, as a man of faith. Not indeed without my infidelities; no more than Paul am I "already perfect" (Phil 3:12). And still, what a congregation must sense in my sermon is that these are not disembodied words, syllables floating in space, eternal verities in a Platonic world of "ideas." I have to, I must want to, preach in such a way that men and women before me can react: "Wow! He really believes this stuff. He actually believes that Jesus is alive and well, that to save your life you must lose it, that to live humanly you ought to love God above all else, love your sisters and brothers as Jesus loves them. The words are flowing from his life; he seems to be suffering to live them."

This involves conversion, a ceaseless turning to Christ. Not a process which a preacher simply recommends to a needy congregation. No. When I repeat the Baptist's "Repent" (Mt 3:2), I ought, like John, to be "preaching in the wilderness" (v. 1). In my wilderness, Calvin Klein may have replaced "camel's hair," a Lacoste belt John's "leather girdle," beef fondue his "locusts and wild honey" (v. 4). Such details, though not impertinent to conversion, can be incidental. What is indispensable, if preaching is to contribute to congregational conversion, is that my homily be part and parcel of my constant turning to Christ. In a word, to promote conversion, my homily should proceed from conversion, my increasing surrender, in obedience, to God's demands on me.

It's a liberating experience, believe me. I no longer mount the pulpit as one who dwells with God in light inaccessible. But genuinely liberating only if, like St. Paul, I continually carry the marks of Christ's passion in my flesh. Only if I share in some way the poverty of the poor to whom I preach so trippingly the poverty of Christ. Only if the love I would have lavished on wife and children is spent on all the loveless and unlovable who cry out to me. Only if my vow of obedience delivers me from a damnable preoccupation with my own wants, my own good pleasure, my own satisfaction, rather than the will of God and the agonizing needs of God's people.

A nerve-tingling question: Do my people hear a pilgrim who walks beside them, a man of faith who loves God and them with a crucifying passion, a constant convert ever reaching out to touch the hem of God's garment? If they do, once they do, then all sorts of mountains will move, all manner of mulberry trees will be uprooted and planted in God's sea.

Immaculate Heart of Mary Seminary
Winona, Minnesota
November 8, 1993

WEDDING HOMILIES

23
LOVE IS A FLAME OF THE LORD
Wedding Homily 1

- Song of Songs 2:8-10, 14, 16a; 8:6-7a
- Romans 12:1-2, 9-13
- Matthew 5:13-16

You have just listened to the Word of God; now you are expected to listen to the word of a mere man. Fortunately, the two "words," though not the same, are not totally different. For my own words take their rise from the three passages Chris and Meg have plucked from God's Book. Let me try to deepen your understanding of what you have heard, suggest how pertinent it all is to the life-together which this dear couple begins today.

I

Some of you may be surprised that Meg and Chris have selected for their first biblical reading a passage from the Song of Songs, the Canticle of Canticles. Surprised because what the Song of Song sings is a theme that rarely reaches the Catholic pulpit: human sexual love. I know, Jewish thought has treated this biblical book as an allegory for the marriage between the Lord and Israel; Christian thinkers down the ages have seen therein the love that blazes between Christ and his Church, or between Christ and the human soul. I do not reject all this, but one thing is clear: In its literal sense the Song sings of the love between a man and a woman.[1] A love at once selfless and sensual, at once a love in spirit and in flesh.

No need for embarrassment. I rejoice that the Song of Songs sings of such love. For in this way we have God's own word, God's own guarantee, that the love of man and woman, sexual love included, is a good thing. Not indeed everything that in our time passes for love, from the one-night stands to TV's "Love Boat." Rather, the kind of love for which a God of love shaped man and woman as similar but not the same. I mean the love that engages everything that is genuinely human in them, involves the whole person. Where there is always "I and thou" but decreasingly "mine and thine." Where to love is to share, not only what they have but, more importantly, who they are. Where love means not "as long as we like it" but "as long as life shall last." As in the beginning, so now, God looks on what he has made "and indeed it [is] very good" (Gen 1:31).

Wonder of wonders, all this, from initial attraction through sexual oneness to total sharing, all this is not only a good thing. Recall one striking sentence that was read to you from the Song of Songs: The love of man and maid is "a flame of the Lord" (Cant 8:6). What does that mean? It means that genuine oneness between lover and beloved is a sharing in God's white-hot love.[2] This is not something we have in common with brute animals. The way Meg and Chris love each other gives us some idea of how totally and passionately God loves. On every level of their love they share in God's love and they reveal something of what God's love is like.

Little wonder that in the Song the woman cries, "Love is strong as death" (Cant 8:6). The ancient Hebrews represented death almost as if it were a person, pictured death as an unrelenting power; no one escapes it. True love, she declares, is just as powerful, equally strong.

II

Second, Chris and Meg have chosen an intriguing Gospel, awesome. They are to be salt to their earth, light to their world. What can this possibly mean? For this, you must go back to the first century.

In first-century Palestine salt was a must, was irreplaceable. Not yet for Margaritas, but for meat and fish. Not simply to improve their taste, but also to preserve them. It kept them from spoiling, from rotting. And in the one-room cottage of the Oriental peasant, the small dish-like device in which oil was burned, the common-clay oil lamp, was indispensable. Without it life would have been dark indeed. Once the sun went down, the Jew could not have read his "Law of Moses," could not have walked with sure foot and light heart.

What Jesus is telling us is that in large measure the moral well-being of this world, the good state of our society, depends on Jesus' disciples, on you and me. From this day forward Meg and Chris are to be salt together. Their oneness, the quality of their love, should spice married life and preserve it, help bring marriage back to the total lifelong oneness that God designed, bring Christian marriage to St.

Paul's vision, a striking symbol of the love that links Christ and his bride the Church.

The Catholic bishops of this country are dedicating this decade to "Children and Families First."[3] Understandably, for as Pope John Paul II has insisted, "In the Christian view, our treatment of children becomes a measure of our fidelity to the Lord himself."[4] This is something the Teglers have always understood and lived. Back in 1986 I dedicated one of my collections of homilies to Mary Margaret and Albert W. Tegler,

> whose living homilies are 17 children,
> 75 grandchildren,
> 7 great-grandchildren,
> all of whom have learned from them,
> as I too have learned,
> how to wed wisdom to silence as well as to words,
> how to love the unloved as we love ourselves,
> how to give without counting the cost,
> how to fashion a Christlife merry with laughter
> and walk on crutches with grace.

Meg and Chris will surely walk in that family tradition. But not only for their biological children. It is their mission to move their love to the world's children, to America's children. Their love should help restore American family life to what it was before this our day, when every 26 seconds a child runs away from home, every 47 seconds a child is seriously neglected or abused, every 67 seconds a teenager has a baby, every 36 minutes a child is killed or injured by a gun; when 5.5 million children under 12 are hungry; when almost a fourth of American children grow up under a single parent;[5] when a million children sleep on America's streets each night, "scared, cold, hungry, alone, and most of all, desperate to find someone who cares."[6]

The vocation of Christian parents is to respond to the urging of Jesus, "Let the little children come to me, and do not stop them; for it is to such as these that the kingdom of heaven belongs" (Mt 19:14). More children, Meg and Chris, than you can visualize today: the little children born of your flesh and spirit; the little children related to you by bonds of blood; the little children who will beg mutely for your love from staring eyes, empty stomachs, abused bodies.

III

Love for each other, love for God's children—a splendid way to live married life. But, to reach its full potential, such love must be rooted not in humans but in God. Your choice of a passage from St. Paul puts it powerfully: "Present your bodies as a living sacrifice, holy and acceptable to God, which is your spiritual worship. Do not be conformed to this world, but be transformed by the renewing of your minds, so that you may discern what is the will of God—what is good and acceptable and perfect" (Rom 12:1-2).

"Do not be conformed to this world." It is not a blanket indictment of everything that goes on outside Christian living. It is a warning against letting your life, your mind and heart, be molded by the dominant culture—in our time, what sociologists see as a resurgence of late-19th-century rugged individualism, a me-first mentality, where the primary stress is on *my* needs and *my* wants, what *I* like or don't like; where life is the survival of the fittest, and the race is to the swift, the smart, the savage. No, St. Paul declares, "be transformed"; shape your life, shape your self, in the image of Jesus, the Son of God who took our flesh to fashion it like his own. I mean, to shape men and women who prefer giving to getting, being to having, sacrificing to clutching, serving to being served, are ready to love even when loving involves crucifixion.

It is precisely such transformation that married life demands, perhaps more than anywhere else, perhaps more troubling than in any other vocation. For here there are two who have to give, be, sacrifice, serve, love...together...as long as they live. It cannot be done simply by two pair of matching blue eyes. In fact, it would be impossible if we did not have the Gift St. Paul guarantees: "Hope does not disappoint us, because God's love has been poured into [your] hearts through the Holy Spirit who has been given to [you]" (Rom 5:5). The living proof that God loves you, that God will be with you always, that you are already transformed, profoundly changed, is Christ's Holy Spirit, God's Gift of love, within you. God alive in you, in both of you—how can you not begin life, live life, close life as St. Paul exclaimed in wonder: "If [you are] in Christ, there is a new creation; everything old has passed away; see, everything has become new!" (2 Cor 5:17)?

For such transformation to endure, I suggest that a ceaseless center of your wedded life be the Eucharist; for it is in the Eucharist that the Offertory prayer is realized: "By the mystery of this water and wine may we come to share in the divinity of Christ, who humbled himself to share in our humanity." And Eucharist means literally "thanksgiving." With the Eucharist as center, let your life together be an endless thanksgiving. Thanks to a thoughtful Trinity, a God who through uncounted successions of ages and nativities has fashioned you and, against all the odds, has brought you together in such unexpected oneness. Thanks for a God-man who not only died for you but lives in you. Thanks for parents who gave you life and lived for you. Thanks for eyes that can embrace God's fields and streams, hands that can stroke a face or a flower, legs that can challenge the paths of Valley Forge. Thanks for the sun that lights your day and the moon that delights your night. Thanks for music that soothes your spirit and aerobics that trim your waist. Thanks for the garlic Pizza and the Guinness and the Santa Caralina you slurp. Thanks for the wonder of simply being alive, for the miracle of your love.

Thanks to God in a special way for those whose love surrounds you here today. For you dear folk are not spectators at a spectacular. You have come together because in some fashion, large or little, you have helped to shape the love that reaches new heights here. But—a warning—your work is not ended, has only begun. For if Meg and Chris are to live for life what they promise today, a love that gives life to each other and to the crucified images of Christ to whom the recessional will send them, they need this extended family. Not simply for fondue forks and Waterford crystal, Limoges porcelain and Irish linen (but do keep them coming); even more importantly, they need...you. Let your presence here be a promise. A promise that you will be there for them, that you will share with them your strength and your weakness, your laughter and your tears, your prayers and your example. More perhaps than anything else, Meg and Chris need the example of men and women who, for one year or 50, have struggled to live for each other, to live together for others.

And so, when Chris and Meg join hands in a few short moments, I would ask the wedded among you to link your own hands and to murmur softly to each other the words that will bind them till death do them part: "I take you for my wife—I take you for my husband. I promise to be true to you in good times and in bad, in sickness and in health. I will love you and honor you all the days of my life."

It is a wedding gift beyond compare. For in this gift you are giving Meg and Chris...your very selves.

SS. Simon and Jude Church
Philadelphia, Pennsylvania
June 12, 1993

24
ABOVE ALL, CLOTHE YOURSELVES WITH LOVE
Wedding Homily 2

- Tobit 8:5-7
- Colossians 3:12-15
- Mark 10:6-8

You have just heard three passages carefully culled by Mary and Kevin from God's one and only Book. But the passages are so pithy, the delivery was so deft, your concentration on bride and groom so intense, that you may have missed their more profound meaning for this celebration. You see, these texts suggest[1] that, from God's perspective, marriage for Kevin and Mary is a threefold turning: They turn to each other, they turn to the Other, and they turn to the others. A word on each.

I

First, Mary and Kevin turn to each other. Quite obvious, you say. But it's how they turn that is important. St. Paul suggested the how with several specific characteristics: compassion, kindness, humility, patience, forgiveness (Col 3:12-13). But then he added, "Above all, clothe yourselves with love, which binds everything together in perfect harmony" (v. 14). In Mary and Kevin I have been privileged to touch a kind of human loving so sacred, so intimate, that not even a Jesuit dare invade it; I can only share it at a discreet distance. But even when most discreet, I glimpse a love that reveals what God had in mind when he fashioned male and female in God's own image, shaped them for each other.

What do I mean? I mean what Kevin meant when he wrote me that the years appear too short for all he and Mary want to be and do together. "We want to travel together and raise children and write books and build a home and grow old wrapped in each other's arms.

We want to reach 100 and do it all over again." This is not puppy love, adolescent infatuation, Hollywood romance. This is a love that has been seasoned by bittersweet experience in a crazy, souped-up, fast-lane world, experience that has generated not cynicism but loving laughter that lights what Kevin calls "those astonishing green eyes" and Mary terms "those killer blue eyes." This is a love that Mary confesses "makes me better than I am when I am alone," delights her "thinking about all the blueberry pancakes I want to make him on all the Sundays forever."

It is a love that promises to brighten rather than dim with the years. Why? Because it is shaped not of rugged individualists but of two-in-one, where each never ceases to marvel at the wonder of the other, where sharing and communicating is what marriage and life itself are all about. These two sense what the Song of Songs declares: The love of man and maid is "a flame of the Lord" (Cant 8:6). Human love stems from divine love; and human love reveals God's own passionate love, the love that impelled God's only Son to wear our flesh, share our hungers, taste our dying to enrich our living.

II

Love is "a flame of the Lord." In consequence, a second turning. Turned to each other, Kevin and Mary turn to the Other. Here the text from Tobit is entrancing. This Old Testament book has been called "[a] fascinating amalgam of *Arabian Nights* romance, kindly Jewish piety, and sound moral teaching."[2] Be that as it may, in our text the son of Tobit, Tobiah, and his wife Sarah pray together on their wedding night. A lovely prayer from the lips of Tobiah, based on the creation story in Genesis:

> Blessed are you, O God of our fathers,
>   and blessed be your holy and glorious name forever.
>   Let the heavens and all of your creatures bless you.
> You made Adam and gave him Eve his wife
>   as a helper and support.
> From them the race of humankind has sprung.
> You said, "It is not good that the man should be alone;
>   let us make a helper for him like himself."
> (Tob 8:5-6)

That Sarah and Tobiah should turn first to God on their wedding night makes good sense. For if not all marriages are made in heaven, marriage itself is. For it was God who with divine imagination shaped not one human but two. Similar but not the same. Shaped each to image divinity, God's wondrous reality, in his or her own way. Shaped them with spirit and flesh geared to self-giving. Shaped them such that from this wedding of spirit and flesh would issue the fruit of their self-giving, images of themselves, images of God. Shaped them so that in their oneness they might see their Maker more clearly, love more dearly, follow more nearly, until that blessed day when, as Scripture assures us, they will together "see God as God is" (1 Jn 3:2), rest in God's love together days without end.

And so it makes sense that Mary and Kevin begin their life-together-for-life by turning to God. But in a unique way. For this celebration is not just a nice way of "tying the knot," a lovely setting, on a campus with rich memories of college friends and...Patrick Ewing. In this house of God they turn to God by celebrating the central act of Catholic worship, the most remarkable love in human history, when the Son of God in our flesh gave his life so that we might have life and have it in all its richness. Here they begin their life together by receiving together, in their hands, on their tongues, in their flesh and hearts, the Christ of Calvary who died and rose for them, the risen Christ who "always lives to make intercession for them" (Heb 7:25).

Here, Mary and Kevin, is your central act of thanksgiving, the literal meaning of Eucharist. Here, literally and splendidly, you turn to the God who first turned to you—the God who knew you and loved you before the sun first rose in the east. Never forget the First Letter of John: "In this is love, not that we loved God but that God loved us and sent His Son to be the atoning sacrifice for our sins" (1 Jn 4:10).

III

Your love for each other and your love for the Other lead into my third point: your love for the others. On Monday, May 24, two fascinating articles began on the front page of the *Washington Post*. One was authored by Mary Jordan, the other by Kevin Sullivan. I read no significance, no reverse discrimination, into the fact that Kevin's article was positioned *below* Mary's. What is significant because so characteristic is that both articles dealt competently and compassionately with people problems: Mary with a profound segregation of America's urban schools, Kevin with a 49-year-old Riverdale lady suffering from a progressive deterioration of the central nervous system.[3] Whether Mary is moving from West Palm Beach and an alleged rape to Waco and a messiah's disaster, whether Kevin is writing about Capital hockey star Rod Langway "On Thin Ice,"[4] a collector of pink Cadillacs, or a group of women playing bridge together for half a century, they bring to my mind's eye a fresh vision of what Christian marriage involves.

You see, the recessional that will close this Nuptial Mass is not primarily a swift move of the bridal party to the reception before the congregation crowds to the cocktails. The recessional is symbolic. It is, Mary and Kevin, your movement from church to world, from altar to people, from Christ crucified to the crucified images of Christ. My thesis is splendidly summarized in a single sentence by Marian Williamson in her *Return to Love:* "We do not marry each other to escape the world; we marry each other to heal it together."[5]

That mission leaps from the Hebrew prophets. It is summarized in Micah's question, "What does the Lord require of you?" He insists that the Lord answered that question: "Act justly, love steadfastly..." (Mic 6:8). As with the Israelites, so with us. The justice God asks is not simply an ethical construct: Give to each what is due to each, what each person has a strict right to demand, because he or she is a human being, has rights that can be proven from philosophy or have been written into law. Justice is a whole set of relationships that stem from our covenant with God. Like the Israelites, we are to father the fatherless and mother the motherless, house the homeless and show hospitality to the stranger, touch the hopeless with our hope and the loveless with our love, not because they deserve it, but because this is what our commitment to Christ, our covenant with him, demands, and because this is the way God has acted with us. For us as for Israel, such justice is an expression of steadfast love. Not to execute justice is not to worship God.

The point is, your wedded oneness has to go out to the pain that surrounds you, to the fears and tears on the road you travel together, to addle heads and lonely hearts. Not just in global abstraction. I mean this infant born with Down's syndrome, that child hungry for bread and love, those youngsters sexually abused. I mean the tragedy of America's devastated families.

Why you? Because only families can rebuild the human family, where every man, woman, and child is sacred, feels loved. Governments can legislate action; they cannot legislate love; the struggle for equal rights has proved that. Superbly qualified to change hearts are men and women who have experienced love, who realize that profound love involves crucifixion, whose model in loving is the Christ who declared, "There is no greater love than this: to lay down [your] life for [your sisters and brothers]" (Jn 15:13). Such, Mary and Kevin, have been your mothers and fathers, who have lived for you, for seven children and two, have lived for days such as this, life-givers whose genes for self-giving have been transmitted to another generation, to you and your siblings.

What delights me is that you do indeed go out to others—in a way not open to the majority of humans. You live with words—words that make men and women come alive to a whole little world. You uncover the uncommon stories of common and uncommon men and women. You write about them in a style that is attractive, compelling, exciting. You help us to see below the surface, to grasp the comic and the tragic in the human situation. You do it at times with good humor—which Thackeray once defined as a wedding of wit and love. You urge on us an understanding of others that reminds me of an insight expressed many years ago by Meg Greenfield. She stated that, despite ever so many reasons advanced for the calamitous outcome of our venture into Vietnam, one has been totally overlooked: We did not really know who the Vietnamese were. But what I like best is that, however objective you are, your objectivity is not hard, cold; you are not blasé reporters on the outside looking in. You feel deeply; your thoughts throb, your language laughs, your words weep. You link us in compassion with the crucified, help untold thousands of us to walk a few steps in the shoes of the less fortunate.

Such an approach is not only an exciting job; it is a God-given vocation. Through you we learn to live more fully the second great commandment of the Mosaic law and the Christian gospel: Love your sisters and brothers as if they were other selves.

Good friends all: You gather here not as spectators at a spectacular, but as a community of love. For each of you has played a part, featuring or supporting, in the exciting drama, the love story, that touches new heights today. Paradoxically, your role calls for a Brother or Sister Act II.[6] For Kevin and Mary will live their wedded life not in some primeval paradise but on a planet where in mortal combat life struggles with death, love with hate, hope with despair, compassion with competition, Godlikeness with godlessness. If they are to turn, ceaselessly and for life, to each other, to the Other, and to the others, they need not only the generous graces God promises them through today's sacrament; they need the unique gift that is you. Concretely, the assurance that you will always "be there" for them—your hands and hearts and homes, your fidelity and fortitude, your love.

In a special way, they need the example of men and women who for one year or 50, through anguish and ecstasy, have lived for each other, for God, and for the crucified images of Christ. That is why, a few moments from now, when Kevin and Mary join their hands for life,

I would ask the wedded among you to join your own hands and murmur with them the words that once transformed your existence, words that must mean so much more today: "I take you for better for worse, for richer for poorer, in sickness and in health. I will love you and honor you all the days of my life."

No more precious a gift can you give this dear couple. For you are giving them...yourselves.

Dahlgren Chapel
Georgetown University
July 3, 1993

25
WITHOUT LOVE I AM...NOTHING
Wedding Homily 3

- Genesis 1:26-28, 31a
- 1 Corinthians 12:31–13:8a
- Matthew 22:35-40

Last year, in a *Time* review of a French movie, *A Heart in Winter*, Richard Corliss wrote:

> American movies are all talk, no listen. Jabber jabber, feint feint—conversation is combat, a schoolyard dissing contest.... In real life, and in French movies, people pretend to get along when they talk. They keep things light, genial, talking around the issues that burn them up inside. Some love affairs never begin because people are afraid to reveal what they feel. "I love you" is so hard to say. Some marriages can last a lifetime on the tacit agreement that hostilities will go unexpressed. The static is in the silences.[1]

In the selections they have plucked from God's own Book, Amy and Jeff have told us that they are willing, even anxious, to say "I love you." So then, let's plumb these passages from Scripture, uncover what they have revealed to Jeff and Amy, what they might say to us who love them more than a little. Three passages, three ideas: (1) God's love for Amy and Jeff; (2) the love of Jeff and Amy for each other; (3) their love for the less fortunate of their sisters and brothers in Christ.

I

First, the passage from Genesis. It is particularly pertinent here today because it is God telling Amy and Jeff, "I love you." Recall, in a bit more detail, what happened that glorious day in the Garden of Eden. Let your imagination run loose. Picture the first man ever, shaped by God in the very likeness of God. Picture him delighting in the universe the Lord God had shaped for him: relishing the warmth of day and the cool of night, in awe at the sun and the moon and the stars, letting rich loam trickle through his fingers, wide-eyed at playful dolphins and regal eagles, at prowling panthers and graceful swans. See him munching juiced-up apples, cracking coconuts for his Piña Colada, breathing the fragrance of luxuriant lilies, skinny-dipping in sparkling streams.

Perfect, no? No. Something was missing, something even the man could not imagine. God put a divine finger on it: "It is not good that the man should be alone; I will make him a partner fit for him" (Gen 2:18). Now notice what our imaginative God does. First God brings to Adam animals from the forest, birds from the sky. Why? "To see what he would call them" (v. 19). To "call" them, to "name" them, this meant to recognize their nature, understand what they really are. And Adam realizes that no one of these, not all of them together, like to him though they are, are like enough to him. In none of them does he find "a partner fit for him" (v. 20). No animal, no winged creature, none corresponds to him, can play the partner, the helper, God has in mind. And so the man remains alone.

But not for long. The way the inspired poetic author saw it, the Lord God cast a deep sleep upon Adam, and while he slept God shaped from his rib another creature. As soon as he brought this creature to Adam, the man saw her for what she was, cried in ecstasy, "At last this one [three times he shouts it, 'this one'] is bone of my bones and flesh of my flesh.... That is why a man leaves his father and mother and clings to his wife, and the two of them become one flesh" (vv. 23-24).

Don't be alarmed: In point of fact, Adam did not lose a rib, he gained a wife. Someone wonderfully like him, yet strikingly different. She too in God's likeness, but in her own wondrous way. Free like him, free to love. Made for him, as he had been made for her.

Through billions of years, dear Amy and Jeff, that scene has now come down to you. God's love for you? Why, two fresh images of God, like God each in your own way. Unique likenesses of God, for you were not fashioned in a heavenly factory; there is simply no one quite the same as you.

II

Which brings me to my second point, the love of Amy and Jeff for each other. You see, what God's love did in bringing Adam and Eve together has its contemporary counterpart in the miracle that brought

Amy and Jeff together. Again, let your imaginations roam, this time for real. Recall a scenario that is set in the late 80s. Take a lass from Kenosha and a lad from Gaithersburg; set them down at the same Jesuit college, one of 28, in a single city, Milwaukee. Focus one in business, the other in education. Mix them with 11,776 other students from across the U.S.[2] Put him manning a desk in one residence hall when the other just happens to drop in. Words pass for the first time, two sets of blue eyes meet, and the rest is history. For surprises, Eden had nothing on Milwaukee.

In this context, Amy and Jeff, the passage from Paul's first letter to the Christians of Corinth should be scotch-taped to your refrigerator door. For Paul not only tells you that without love you are nothing... simply no thing, unreal. Paul tells you what escapes much of America's media: what that four-letter word "love" should mean. For married love is a tough love; like life itself, it makes heavy demands.

Paul tells us that love is patient—not fretful, irritable, foot-tapping, finger-biting, clock-watching. Paul tells us that love is kind, gentle—not cold-eyed, rough-spoken, thin-lipped. Love doesn't envy the other's success, does not resent the other's friends, is rarely if ever rude or boorish. Love is not egotistical, stubborn, does not insist that only his or her way can ever be the right way. Love rejoices when the other turns out to be right, whether about healthcare or the death penalty, even the Brewers or the Pirates. Paul tells us that love endures simply everything—from wet bathing trunks in the shower through financial stress to life-threatening disease.

Lust is easy; it's love that is tough. In my experience, living together for 50 years is a living miracle; I have discovered only one thing more difficult: living alone. And what makes it possible is not a how-to guide, a set of cookbooks and sex manuals. Paul captured it in his letter to the Christians of Rome: "...hope does not disappoint us, because God's love has been poured into our hearts through the Holy Spirit that has been given to us" (Rom 5:5).

It is not only your wonderfully human love that will keep your love alive, keep you talking when disagreement threatens to drive you to sullen silence, keep you forgiving despite your very human hurts. Surrounding that, impregnating that, deepening that, is God's love for you as man and wife. God's love. Not somewhere in outer space; God within you, God refusing to forsake you even if you forsake God, God ever faithful to a divine promise: to be with you days without end.

III

My third point: This love that links Amy and Jeff simply must go out to others. You see, the recessional that closes this Eucharist is not a swift way to the Pfister Hotel, before we selfish folk get to the bar. The recessional is impressively symbolic. As Amy and Jeff move down the aisle man and wife, think of it not so much as a triumphant procession, rather as their movement from church to world, from altar to people, from Christ crucified on Calvary to the images of Christ crucified on our streets. An insightful woman psychologist stressed this strongly more than a decade ago:

> A love that is not for more than itself will die—the wisdom of Christian tradition and the best we know from psychology both assure us of this truth. It is often very appropriate at the early stages of a relationship that the energy of romance and infatuation exclude the larger world from our vision. But over the long haul an intimate relationship...which doesn't reach outward will stagnate.[3]

That is why the passage Amy and Jeff have chosen from Matthew's Gospel is so pertinent—the second great commandment of the law and the gospel, the commandment Jesus said is like loving God: "You shall love your neighbor as yourself" (Mt 22:39). Now this is not a psychological balancing act: As much or as little as you love yourself, so much or so little shall you love others. No. Careful Scripture scholars have told us what it meant on the lips of Jesus: You shall love each sister, each brother, like another "I." Especially the less fortunate, the oppressed, the downtrodden, the marginalized: You shall love them as if you were standing in their shoes.

You have already touched some of the crucified individually; from now on, you will touch them together. Especially the children. No need to fly to Rwanda, where half a million children have been orphaned by the butchery of war. Wherever you strike roots, one of every five children will look at you with empty, vacant eyes. Hungry for bread indeed, hungrier still for a word or look or touch that tells them they are loved, somebody cares.

A final word—a word I refuse to resist in so love-filled an atmosphere. You are not here as spectators, the way you might have joyed or wept when Brazil "outfooted" Italy last Sunday.[4] You are here because each one of you, without exception, has played some part— feature or supporting—in the love that reaches a high point this morning. My point is, your role has not ended; it will never end. For Amy and Jeff will live their love not on a fantasy island but on an earth where love mingles with hate, belief struggles against cynicism, hope all too often ends in despair, where death never takes a holiday. And they must live their love when the wonder of the other gives way to routine, when the laughter of college and courtship struggles against what we laughingly call "reality," when there is danger of static in their silences.

Wedded love cannot subsist without support. God's grace Jeff and Amy can count on; but it is precisely your love that can be, should be, part of God's grace over their life together—your presence to them even at a distance, your readiness to share of your heart, your ceaseless prayer for happiness beyond compare. One special support they need perhaps more critically than any other. I mean the example of men and women here today who, for one year or 50, have lived the love you vowed through good times and bad, in poverty and plenty, in sickness and in health, through all the bittersweet of wedded oneness—you who tell them without words, by your sheer presence here together, that it can be done, that with God all things are possible. And so, when Amy and Jeff join their hands and hearts a few moments from now, I would ask the wedded among you to join your own hands and murmur once again the words that gave you to each other uniquely, exclusively, as long as life pulses within you.

I can think of no greater gift—not Wedgwood ware or Tiffany glass—you can offer this day to Amy and Jeff. For in this gift, in your daily life of sacrificial love, you are giving this dear couple...yourselves.

Gesu Church
Milwaukee, Wisconsin
July 23, 1994

26
AS JESUS LOVED
Wedding Homily 4

- Genesis 1:26-28, 31
- 1 Corinthians 12:31—13:8
- John 15:9-12

Today a little slice of history is being shaped before your eyes. History human and divine. Thirty-six years ago, in this church, I was privileged to receive the wedding vows of Suzanne Faubert and Philip Briguglio. From that marriage three delightful daughters have descended. Twelve years ago, in this church, I was privileged to receive the vows that linked Laura in endless love to Peter Bilodeau. Eight years ago, in this church, I was privileged to receive the vows that joined Jeanne once and always to Richard Crawford. And today, in this same church, I shall be privileged to receive the vows that, please God, will wed Elizabeth to Scott Fleming in undying oneness.

Now these are not sheer dates, another item for Ripley's *Believe It or Not*. Today the thrilling facet of this history is that once again the history is enveloped in mystery: the mystery-laden reality we call love. This mystery Elizabeth and Scott have opened to us in the three readings they have lovingly plucked from God's own Book, from the Word of God. For through these three passages they have suggested to us in swift succession three profound truths: (1) God's own dream for wedded love, (2) the human reality that imperils this love, and (3) what makes such love possible despite the perils.

I

First, God's own dream for wedded love. Incredibly imaginative, as Genesis tells it. For a brief moment, relive with me that scene in Eden's garden. Two short sentences that should send pleasurable shivers down our spines. The first sentence, "God created humankind

125

in [God's] image" (Gen 1:27). Very simply, God made us like God. True, Genesis does not reveal precisely what that startling sentence means. And so for centuries Scripture scholars and theologians have spilled oceans of ink over this basic truth: God made you and me images of divinity. How do we resemble God? Is it because we can think? Is it because we are free to choose? Is it because, as God is ruler of the universe, we are rulers of earth? More and more I like to believe we are like God especially because we are made to reflect, to image, to mirror a God who is Love.

In God's image. But that sentence is completed by a sentence just as startling: "Male and female God created them" (1:27). Our Lord God shaped not some abstract image of God, not one single image of God. God had in mind, God actually shaped, two humans similar but not the same. Similar because each would image God, each would be a reflection of the Creator, each would be gifted with the grace to love. But not the same, for man and woman would mirror God each in his or her own way: a male way and a female way. And in imaging God, each would be attracted to the other, would find in the other something not just wonderfully human but specifically divine.

This, I believe, Scott and Elizabeth have begun to experience. Not learned it in a classroom; they have discovered it each in the other. Not only some chemistry (which is indeed there); rather God's freely given grace. The kind of grace that kept Elizabeth alive when it seemed her birthing would be her dying. The kind of grace that brought Erie PA and Alexandria VA together when Jimmy the Greek would have taken those odds off the board. The grace that made them see each in the other something so special no preacher can express it in words. The grace to look into each other's eyes and discover...love. God's love and their own.

II

Second, the human reality that imperils such love. You heard the rapturous phrases with which St. Paul described the most genuine kind of love. "Love is patient; love is kind; love is not envious or boastful or arrogant or rude. It does not insist on its own way; it is not irritable or resentful; it does not rejoice in wrongdoing, but rejoices in the truth. It bears all things, believes all things, hopes all things, endures all things. Love never ends" (1 Cor 13:4-8a).

But between those lines is the hidden reality. Love is indeed patient and kind, but lovers can be impossibly impatient, cuttingly unkind. For some mysterious reason, we continue to savage the people we love, yes abuse them, ravage them, destroy them. Love may not be envious, but lovers over the centuries have been insanely jealous: "That smile is reserved for me." Love may not insist on its own way, but lovers without number have felt they know what is best for the other—in politics and religion, in diet and even sports: "You knew when I married you that Monday night is for pro football." Love may not be irritable or resentful, but under pressure lovers get terribly thin-skinned, sulk over every smallest slight, react harshly to the slightest provocation: "I don't like your friends, and I never will."

In my experience, the villain is...time. Time takes its toll not only of our bodies but of our emotions, our reactions. With the years we take our dearest for granted. The gentle kiss that greeted each dawn becomes a hasty peck on parting. The hurts we once shared so generously, now we clam up: "I'll be all right; just leave me alone." The man or woman who only yesterday was unique in my life is often lost in a crowd, in a business. The wonder we spied in the other, the smile that lit the landscape, the eyes that spoke of profound caring, the touch that made us tremble all over—these get lost in the rush we call reality.

America's experience—a 50-percent divorce rate—tells us vividly that it is extraordinarily difficult to live with one other person for 30, 40, 50 years. I know only one life still more difficult: *not* living with one other person.

III

All of which summons up my third point. Wedded life, Paul's paean, his hymn of praise to love, would be a mission impossible, an impossible dream, if Scott and Elizabeth had to achieve it by themselves, by sheerly personal effort: their high IQs, their Doublemint smiles, their blue eyes, their Schwarzenegger wills. Here is where the Gospel they selected takes center stage, the words of Jesus the eve before he died for us: "This is my commandment, that you love one another as I have loved you" (Jn 15:12).

To love as Jesus loved—this is not only his command. It is a promise—a promise that the God who shaped them for love, the Christ who died for love of them, will enable them to love as Jesus loved. This is why we celebrate their love in a house of God, before an altar of sacrifice, rather than in a forest glen, on a mountaintop, on the shores of the Chesapeake Bay. Today's ceremony should symbolize, should remind us of, St. Paul's exciting declaration to the Christians of Ephesus: "We are God's work of art [God's poetry, God's masterpiece], created in Christ Jesus to live the good life as from the beginning God meant us to live it" (Eph 2:10).

Elizabeth and Scott: Marriage is not simply another milestone in your life. It is indeed that, but it is more. It should be the beginning of a fresh intimacy with God—a God who is working ceaselessly to achieve in both of you together God's dream back in Eden's garden: that you become increasingly one in three ways: one with each other, one with the Other, one with the others whose lives you will touch day after day. Impress this on your minds and hearts: The God who made you male and female, the God who shaped you like God, who infused in you the power to love, this God makes it possible for you not only to endure each other for one year or 50, but to grow in your love, to be more utterly in love in 2044 than in 1994.

I have seen it, I see it still: men and women unbelievably faithful to each other, to their sisters and brothers, to their God. But not with a marital push button. Simply husbands and wives, like so many here today, who not only live together but are alive together, pray together and even golf together, laugh together and cry together—above all, love God together. A God who is alive not somewhere in outer space but deep within them.

Good friends all: I began with one family; let me end with the other. For Elizabeth and Scott have a heritage to complement the Briguglio experience. I mean a woman who, like Mary of Nazareth, has felt the sword of sorrow time and again. I mean a wife who loved and lost not one husband but two; a mother who welcomed two more children to her own five; a lover of our Lord who has experienced crucifixion in her flesh, and in her own way has prayed with Jesus in the garden of his agony, "Father, if you are willing, remove this cup from me; yet, not my will but yours be done" (Lk 22:42).

At a time when the medical profession is anxious to improve the genes that predetermine tomorrow's generation, Scott and Elizabeth can thank God for parents who have transmitted to them God's love and their own; can thank God for siblings who have shown in reality joyful and grim what it means to love as Jesus loved. Truly, "Greater love than this no one has, to give one's life for those one loves" (cf. Jn 15:13). Such, Elizabeth and Scott, such is your heritage. Such, please God, such will be your future.

Holy Trinity Church
Washington, D.C.
November 26, 1994

MEDLEY

27
TO PREPARE HIS WAYS
Feast of the Birth of John the Baptist

- Isaiah 49:1-6
- Acts 13:22-26
- Luke 1:57-66

As we go forth to preach the just word,[1] I want to focus my homily on three persons: (1) John the Baptist, (2) Aleksandr Solzhenitsyn, and (3) a priest of Dubuque.

I

First, John the Baptist. The prophecy of his father is splendidly pertinent here: "You, child, will be called the prophet of the Most High; for you will go before the Lord to prepare his ways" (Lk 1:76). He was not the Messiah. This he made clear to the crowds who thought he might be. "One who is more powerful than I is coming; I am not worthy to untie the thong of his sandals" (3:16). John was a prophet, a person sent by God to proclaim God's word—here God's Word in our flesh.

John's whole life, John's short life, was spent going before Jesus to prepare his ways. I find it thrillingly symbolized when Mary "went with haste" to visit her kinswoman Elizabeth. For it was then—as soon as Elizabeth heard Mary's greeting—that "the child leaped for joy in her womb" (Lk 1:41, 44). Already one more powerful than John had come...and the infant John sensed it.

What was John's message? A message as harsh as his garb and his diet. "Repent, for the kingdom of heaven has come near" (Mt 3:2). Repent. The Greek word means "change your mind," "change your thinking," "turn about," "return," "be converted." John was telling his fellow Jews to reform their lives, to return to the way of life demanded by the covenant between God and Israel, to be faithful to the promise of their fathers, "All that the Lord has spoken we will do, and we will be obedient" (Exod 24:7), to be faithful to the "new covenant" described in Jeremiah, "I will write [my law] upon their hearts; and I will be their God, and they shall be my people" (Jer 31:31, 33).

A harsh message indeed, but paradoxically humane; for John was asking his compatriots to be all they were called to be: the people of God's predilection, of God's special love. And like so many of the prophets, he raised hackles, roused anger, generated hatred. Even King Herod, who "feared John, knowing that he was a righteous and holy man" (Mk 6:20), could not protect him against the wiles of his unlawful wife. She asked for John's head on a platter...and she got it.

II

Second, Aleksandr Solzhenitsyn. Several weeks ago Solzhenitsyn returned to Moscow. Two decades in a sylvan Vermont retreat had been spent preparing for the death of communism and nurturing his own vision of a new Russia. Now 75, this survivor of eight years in the Gulag reached Moscow via a long cross-country train trip, stopping in town after town to greet the locals and listen to their griefs and gripes. What is his message? Listen to a summary in *Time* magazine: "Solzhenitsyn's message to Russians can be summed up in one word: Repent! He believes deeply that Russia cannot move into the future until it has exorcised its communist past."[2]

Like John the Baptist...Repent! Change your way of looking at things. Turn to a whole new way of living. But, as with John, so with Aleksandr: The call to repentance has not been uniformly applauded.

> So far, Solzhenitsyn has been a voice literally crying in the wilderness. His call for Russians to set their sights on higher things has been welcomed by enthusiastic crowds in the hinterlands, but he faces a much tougher audience in Moscow. Few urban sophisticates have time anymore for the kitchen conversations about the Russian soul that were a staple of intellectual life when Solzhenitsyn first lived in the country. A savage commentary in the daily *Nezavisimaya Gazeta* proposed what to do with this troubling revivalist preacher: "Give him mothballs! And more mothballs! And put him to rest!"[3]

III

Third, a priest of Dubuque—each one of you. Unless I am horribly mistaken, no one of you is the Messiah. Like John, you are a prophet of the Lord; you have been anointed by the Lord to proclaim his Word; you go before the Lord to prepare his ways. And the Lord's Word, the Lord's ways, have, I trust, become increasingly clear to you during this unique week.

The Word of the Lord which you must proclaim to your people is not a sheer me-and-Jesus spirituality. Oh yes, your people must love their Lord with all their heart and soul, all their mind and strength. This is indeed "the greatest and first commandment" (Mt 22:38). Unless they love the Lord above every creature on earth, they are less than Christian. Central to their Christian existence is the risen Christ: Christ in the Word proclaimed, Christ in the Eucharist celebrated, Christ in every sacrament from the first immersion to the final oiling, Christ within them, Christ active in every last fragment of his universe.

And still, Jesus proclaimed a commandment he said is "like the first: You shall love your neighbor as yourself" (v. 39). Loving the neighbor is like loving God. And to love the neighbor as yourself, Scripture scholars tell us, is not a psychological balancing act: As much or as little as you love yourself, so much or so little shall you love your neighbor. No, to love your sisters and brothers as yourself is to love them as if you were standing in their shoes.

Such is the biblical justice that must be etched in the hearts of our people: fidelity to relationships imposed by the covenant Christ cut with us in his blood. Not what a sister or brother deserves; rather, how God wants them treated in a covenant where God's unique Son poured out his life for each. "This is my commandment, that you love one another as I have loved you" (Jn 15:12). Even, therefore, unto crucifixion. Only then will they—and we—live the evangelizing mission imposed by each and every baptism, the mission Paul VI proclaimed in 1975:

> Evangelization cannot be complete unless account is taken of the links between the gospel and the concrete personal and social life of men and women.... In proclaiming liberation and ranging herself with all who suffer and toil for it, the Church cannot allow herself or her mission to be limited to the purely religious sphere while she ignores the temporal problems of the human person.... The Church considers it highly important to establish structures which are more human, more just, more respectful of the rights of the person, less oppressive and coercive....[4]

Like the Baptist in Judea, like Solzhenitsyn in Moscow, you will not be a prophet by acclamation in your parish. When you preach a Christianity that rises above what people deserve, ears will be stopped. The "preferential option for the poor" has yet to receive a Catholic "academy award." Still, not only may you take comfort in the growing millions of Catholics who live for others, who play Christ to their sisters and brothers; your strength, your grace, is rooted in God's own revealing Word through the prophet Isaiah:

> Is not this the fast that I choose:
>   to loose the bonds of injustice,
>   to undo the thongs of the yoke,
> to let the oppressed go free,
>   and to break every yoke?
> Is it not to share your bread with the hungry,
>   and bring the homeless poor into your house;
> when you see the naked, to cover them,
>   and not to hide yourself from your own flesh?
> Then your light shall break forth like the dawn,
>   and your healing shall spring up quickly....
> Then you shall call, and the Lord will answer;
>   you shall cry for help, and He will say, Here I am.
>   (Isa 58:6-9)

Loras College
Dubuque, Iowa
June 24, 1994

28

THE POOR WILL NEVER FORGIVE YOU UNLESS....
Feast of St. Vincent de Paul

- Zechariah 8:1-8
- Luke 9:46-50

Back in 1947, a moving motion picture contained a sentence I have never forgotten. The film was titled *Monsieur Vincent*—the story of St. Vincent de Paul, fabulous apostle of charity. At one point Vincent says to his coworkers, "Unless you love, the poor will never forgive you for the bread you give them."

Unless you love.... Let's talk (1) about Vincent and (2) about ourselves.[1]

I

First, Vincent de Paul.[2] Take yourself back to the last decades of the 16th century. Imagine a young native of Gascony, of humble origins—what used to be called "poor but pious parents." His task is to herd the family livestock—cattle, sheep, pigs. Somewhat snobbish: ashamed of a father who limped, who dressed in baggy trousers and foul-smelling sheepskin. Angry with his elders resigned to living conditions he could not countenance. One way "to escape from the mud of his native village"[3] is education for the priesthood. Ordained at 19 or 20, four or five years short of Trent's prescriptions, he searches for a fat place to serve, goes on to finish his seven-year university course with a bachelor's degree in theology. At that point one biographer pictures him as "an efficient, self-reliant, hard-working young man, a little snobbish perhaps, attractive in manner, somewhat easily moved, fundamentally generous but with no outstanding virtues or vices...a good priest in a land where good priests were few... [showing] no signs of being on the highroad to sanctity."[4]

135

Five years ordained, he is captured by pirates, paraded naked through the streets of Tunis, and sold as a slave—first to a fisherman, then to a Muslim alchemist who has spent 50 years searching in vain for the philosophers' stone, finally to an atheistic Frenchman. Two years later he has escaped and made his way to Avignon, "city of the popes," and is looking for a decent benefice.

Not yet 30, Vincent moves from Rome to Paris, where he is to spend almost all of the next 52 years. Just when it seems that his less than sanctifying ambitions are to be realized, his life takes a different direction. The great influence now is Pierre de Bérulle, who had brought St. Teresa's Carmelites of the Reform from Salamanca to Paris and would introduce Philip Neri's Oratorians into France. To Bérulle and his group Vincent is increasingly attracted. He begins to see the grave problems facing the French Church: discipline at a standstill, churches half in ruins, Trent's reforms opposed, the priesthood a mockery and sham, religion neither practiced nor held in honor, the bishop a temporal lord, rich convents and abbeys, priories ruled by Protestants, a youngster made bishop at 11, prelates spending much time at court. It was rare to find a priest who could read or write; some heard confessions without knowing the words of absolution. A canon wrote to him:

> In this diocese the clergy know no discipline, the people know no fear, the priests know neither piety nor charity. The pulpits have no preachers, learning is not honoured, vice is not chastised. Virtue is persecuted and the Church's authority is either hated or despised.... The most scandalous are the most powerful and flesh and blood have taken the place of the Gospel and the spirit of Jesus Christ.[5]

A caustic aphorism current in Provence declared, "If you want to go to hell, make yourself a priest."[6]

The change in Vincent is slow, gradual. He is found more frequently in the Charity Hospital and in the poorer quarters of the city. In a retreat at the Oratory he looks back on his 30 years, asks if all his experiences are intended to have him live as a worldly abbé. At last he makes a promise to God: He will devote his life to service of the poor. In a poor country parish he founds the Association of Charity, self-styled "servants of the poor," women visiting the sick, cooking for them, helping them wash, cheering them up, staying a little longer with those who are alone. More than a hundred *grandes dames* transform Paris' great city hospital (at least 900 patients) from a hell of misery and despair to a haven of hope and love. And it began with a sermon—a sermon so persuasive that it sent 50 housewives speeding to a stricken family with chicken and wine.

Simply to list the shelters he founded and the unfortunates he personally served takes my breath away. There is a halfway house for prisoners condemned to the galleys but too sick to row; for six or seven years he is with the galleys constantly. He makes the rounds of the Paris prisons, where men are "chained to the walls like so many cattle, their bedding vermin-infested straw, their food a totally inadequate ration of black bread."[7] He draws up contracts "for the establishment and maintenance of a number of ecclesiastics, to be chosen by [him],... priests who shall relinquish benefice and office and bind themselves to serve devotedly, completely and disinterestedly the poor people of the country districts...."[8] He even tells his blood brothers and sisters not to expect assistance from him; "and even if I had chests of gold and silver I would not give you anything, for a priest who possesses anything owes it to God and the poor."[9]

At 38 he meets Francis de Sales, arguably the most profound influence on his life. As one biographer puts it, "In Bérulle he found sanctity and bent the knee; in Francis he found a saint and gave him his heart."[10] To converse with Francis is ceaselessly a source of overflowing joy. He follows Francis in insisting on love as the all-powerful weapon, Francis' conviction that love alone can shake the walls of Geneva. His very preaching sets out to persuade by loving people, and by loving them getting people to love him and his apostolate. Francis even bequeaths to a moody and depressed Vincent something of his own serenity. "I was completely delivered from my black humour."[11]

The priests of Vincent's Congregation of the Mission labor among the country poor, impoverished in spirit and flesh. Tenant farmers, share croppers, journeymen—bare survival is their hope. The entire economic structure of France depends on them, yet on them falls the major portion of the taxes. Wars wipe out whole villages; undisciplined soldiers loot defenseless, ill-fed peasants. His religious Daughters of Charity tend the helplessly sick and the plague-stricken, wounded soldiers and galley slaves.

The stories are legion. But behind it all is a profound interior life. He begs the Daughters of Charity to see Christ in the disadvantaged they serve: the sick and the galley slave, the foundling and the poverty-stricken. He tells them that their love for God is proven not by consolation in prayer or emerging from prayer speaking like angels, but in working for God, suffering, seeking the scattered flock—in a word, love in action. And not only in France. He tells his priests that their field of work is "all the inhabited parts of the earth."[12]

Even in his 80s Vincent is caring for war orphans, poor farmers, prisoners, refugees, returning soldiers. But the time comes when his legs fail him, he can no longer celebrate Mass, is completely immobilized. For several months he has had to be carried to his beloved poor—but still with something of his mocking irony: "Now I am a great lord, the equal of bishops."[13] At 4:30 on Monday morning, September 27, 1660, his final agony begins; before dawn he leaves Paris for ever.

II

And what of us? Let me suggest how intimately Vincent de Paul can touch all we are and do. I mean our situation, our response, and our motivation.

First, our situation. As I ran through the life of Monsieur Vincent, I was dismayed. Not primarily over the dreadful, frightful world he encountered; more agonizingly still, how closely our world parallels his. I know, in so many areas we can say to our world, "You've come a long way, baby." We are stronger and live longer; we can walk on the moon and talk to outer space; we can replace hearts and displace dictators; we can learn more in a day than the 16th century learned in a lifetime. And yet, the poor we still have with us, but in even more massive numbers; wars still bloody our earth, but now with the potential of destroying it; the sick still overrun our hospitals and mental institutions; racism, color, still divides our peoples, but now in far more subtle and complex ways; drugs destroy our bodies to a degree Vincent could never have imagined; women are still second-class citizens around the globe.

Our response, specifically in Preaching the Just Word? Several years ago, creative Old Testament scholar Walter Brueggemann addressed what he called the problem of "scandal" in the preaching of social, political, and economic issues.

> In Luke 7, after John the Baptist raises his christological question through his disciples whether Jesus is the Christ, and after Jesus answers with specificity that "the blind see, the lame walk, lepers are cleansed, the dead are raised, and the poor rejoice," Jesus adds, "blessed is the one who is not scandalized by me" (v. 23).... The theological scandal of biblical faith, especially when rendered into political, economic issues, is indeed upsetting.
>
> How is a pastor to give voice to this scandal in a society that is hostile to it, in a church that is often unwilling to host the scandal, and when we ourselves as teachers and pastors of the church are somewhat queasy about the scandal as it touches our

own lives? How can the radical dimension of the Bible as it touches public reality be heard in the church?[14]

This week is a succinct, sustained effort to suggest how we may, how we must, "give voice to this scandal." It insists that Scripture reveals a God who had in mind a people, a human family, a community of persons, a body genuinely one. As Vatican II declared, "God...has willed that all men and women should constitute one family."[15] "God did not create man and woman for life in isolation, but for the formation of social unity."[16] This project looks back to centuries of social teaching often called "the Church's best-kept secret." It asserts that the liturgy at its best is a powerful force for social justice, not because it solves specific issues but because it makes us aware of our deep-rooted selfishness, turns us inside out, makes for conversion. Above all, it confronts the widespread conviction that justice and the pulpit are incompatible, proclaims that social justice is the Christian effort to live out the second great commandment of the gospel: Love your brothers and sisters as if they were other selves—in fact, love them as Jesus has loved you.

And precisely there is our motivation, the motive force that drove Vincent de Paul. Knowledge is important, but knowledge is not enough. Enthusiasm is expected, but enthusiasm is not enough. The Christian drive is the ultimate four-letter word: love. "Unless you love, the poor will never forgive you for the bread you give them." It's not easy. For the poor—all those who hunger and thirst for bread and justice and love—are often the less attractive in an America that worships youth, strength, and beauty. The poor inhabit a way of life we rarely if ever share. The poor see us as living on a different planet. Somehow they must come to see you and me as his contemporaries saw Vincent: men who care for the careworn, agonize over the AIDS-afflicted, look into despairing eyes and weep, touch shriveled flesh with God's love and our own.

Good St. Vincent, help us to live the Song of Solomon: "The fire of love is a flame of Yahweh" (Cant 8:6), a share in the Lord's white-hot love.[17] Ask Christ to turn us inside out, to make each of us a new creation. Show us how to preach with fire in our bellies: indignation over injustice, compassion for the crucified, sorrow for our self-indulgence. Teach us how to persuade by loving. Monsieur Vincent, pray for us, for we are poorer than we know.

The Mount Community Center
Atchison, Kansas
September 27, 1993

29
HERE I AM, KNOCKING AT THE DOOR
Feast of St. Alphonsus Rodriguez

- Ephesians 6:10-18
- Luke 14:1, 7-11

"Here I am, knocking at the door" (Rev 3:20). My story this evening is a tale of two doormen—perhaps a third.

I

Several days ago, I happened to be standing in front of a fashionable D.C. hotel. I was waiting for several friends. For want of something better to do, I focused on the doorman. His name I never discovered; but no matter. Braided and beribboned like the dictator of a banana republic, he dominated this half acre of our nation's capital. Majestically he moved from entrance to curb; peremptorily he whistled for a standing cab; with a flourish he opened the doors of a stretch limo; with courtesy he greeted a politician by name; with dignity he saluted what seemed near royalty. Every so often a greenback would glide gracefully from hand to hand—a transaction hardly noticed by what an Afro-American friend once called "the éternal Revenue." This was our doorman's turf—and he knew it.

II

Back home at Gonzaga, I hunkered down to a homily.[1] Here too I focused on a doorman. A different type indeed. This was a doorman of the 16th century, doorman of a Jesuit college in Palma, on an island called Majorca, off the coast of Spain. Doorman for nigh onto four decades.

His name I knew: Alphonsus Rodriguez. Not always a doorman.

He had been a student of the Jesuits, but was compelled to leave school when his cloth-merchant father died. He had taken over the business, but heavy taxes brought the business to a smashing halt. He had married, happily, sired three children, but then in swift tragic succession son Gaspar died, daughter Maria died, wife Maria died, young Alphonsus died. A failure in his own eyes, prayer and penance stimulated in him a burning yearning to serve God. How? As a Jesuit priest. But he was told in no uncertain terms that he was too old, insufficiently educated, too frail for the rugged regimen of Jesuit priesthood. Two years of education took care of sheer knowledge, and once more he craved admission, this time as priest or brother. But all-wise examiners still found him less than robust and carrying all too many years (he was all of 37). Thanks be to God, a Father Provincial overrode the examiners. We are told—legend or fact, I know not—that the same Provincial said: If Alphonsus is not cut out to be a priest or brother, he may enter to become a saint.

Four decades a doorman. No resplendent garb, only a simple black robe. No authority, only service. Open the college door cordially to visitors, find faculty or students wanted in the parlors, deliver messages, run errands, give alms to the needy, comfort troubled youngsters.

Terribly humdrum, routine? Four decades in a rut? Apparently not. His secret? It comes from his own lips, his own pen. Each time the bell rang, Alphonsus looked at the door and imagined. Imagined what? Imagined that the bell ringer was God—God asking entrance. On the way he would repeat again and again, "I'm coming, Lord." No respecter of persons, save the person of the Lord. Whoever came to the door—the high and mighty or the lowly and powerless, the bold and beautiful or the humble and unremarkable—each visitor met, and enjoyed, the smile Alphonsus kept for God. For in each who came to the door Alphonsus saw the same God, heard one only voice, "Here *I* am, knocking at the door." This was God's turf—and he knew it.

Little wonder that students rang his bell time and again. Some confused, for counsel; some depressed, for courage; some desperate, for prayers. Do you need a concrete example? When Alphonsus was 72, an adolescent came to the college in Majorca. He was afire for God, wanted above all else to serve, but was puzzled: How serve? How best give of himself? Where? He rang Alphonsus' bell; the two became fast friends; they met time and again on the college grounds, talked about prayer, about holiness. At Alphonsus' urging, the student volunteered for the missions in South America. In fulfillment of a vow to be "slave forever of the Ethiopians," he labored for life in Cartagena, Colombia, among the black slaves brought from Africa. The student's name? Peter Claver. On one glorious day in 1888, Pope Leo XIII raised Alphonsus and Peter together to the rank of the Church's saints.[2]

III

And what of us? I find in Alphonsus a stimulus not only for Jesuit brothers, but for all who claim to be companions of Ignatius, companions of Jesus. Two reasons for this perhaps surprising declaration.

The first reason leaps out of today's liturgy, from the opening prayer: "Lord our God, in St. Alphonsus, our brother, you have shown us the way to fidelity that leads to joy and peace. May we remain watchful and attentive as companions of Jesus, who became the servant of all." Fidelity. The reality, if not the word, springs equally from his life and from his spiritual writings. One thing only did he want, "that everything I do may be done as it pleases Jesus and his most holy mother, and not in any other way."[3] Fidelity. Here is the word, the reality, that lies at the heart of biblical justice. Not simply ethical justice, giving to each man, woman, and child what each deserves. Over and above that, fidelity to relationships that stem from a covenant. Three relationships that say it all: loving God above all else, treating each sister and brother like another self, and caring reverently for the earth on which we dance so lightly.

The second reason goes back to our text from Revelation: "Here I am, knocking at the door." It is Ignatius' insistence, in the final contemplation of his Spiritual Exercises, "How To Love Like God," that Christ[4] is present and active, works like a laborer, in all of creation, in all of reality, in every human person whose path I cross, who comes knocking at my door. Ignatius compels me to remember that every person I touch, every thing I touch, is already electric with Christ, with his presence, with his activity. Not only in the billions of stars flying the heavens more speedily than light, in over four thousand varieties of roses perfuming our earth, in the shad that ascend the seas from Newfoundland to Florida. More significantly for you and me, Christ "working like a laborer" in the intelligence and love, in the faith and hope, that burrow deep within our sisters and brothers. To Alphonsus as to Ignatius, Christ was real, was alive. Alive not in outer space but in every single work of his loving hands. Alive not only yesterday but at each moment of each creature's existence. The world is charged with the presence of Christ, with the labor of Christ.

In his quiet way Alphonsus reminds me that my privilege and my burden is twofold: first, to be ceaselessly *conscious* of the Christ who labors for me in every creature I encounter, in every image of Christ who knocks at my door; second, to *collaborate*, labor with Christ in simply everything I do. The results, from my experience, can be threefold. (1) The dull can become exciting—yes, even people. (2) Each of us can help transform an acre of God's earth on which so many agonize so heavily. (3) Ignatius and Alphonsus will love us, for we will have captured their vision.

Yes indeed, here God stands, here Christ stands, knocking at our door.

Chapel of Our Lady
Gonzaga High School
Washington, D.C.
October 31, 1994

30

SING A NEW SONG...WITH YOUR LIVES
125th Anniversary of a Parish

- 1 Chronicles 15:3, 16, 19-21, 25
- 1 Corinthians 1:4-9

This afternoon you bring to a close a year of celebration.[1] You do so in striking fashion; for you close on the feast of Corpus Christi and you close if not with a literal bang, certainly with a resounding musical beat. An age-old feast and a new organ. These two events compel me to concentrate not on your impressive past but on your unknown future, compel me to focus on two facets of that future. I mean your Eucharist and your song.

I

First, today's feast focuses on the body and blood of Christ. It reminds us that the central act of Catholic worship is the Eucharist. For the Mass is Catholicism in miniature. Here, if anywhere, the Church Catholic comes together. We do indeed come together for much else: a novena to the Sacred Heart, a prolife rally, a reconciliation service. But the Eucharist is unique. Here alone the whole Catholic world gathers as one—ideally, all 900 million of us; really, perhaps half that number.

It did not begin yesterday. It began one enchanted evening when God-in-flesh commanded his special friends, "Do this in remembrance of me" (Lk 22:20). The effect of that simple command has rarely been expressed more rapturously than by a remarkable Anglican liturgical scholar. Almost a half century ago he penned this precious paragraph:

> Was ever a command so obeyed? For century after century, spreading slowly to every continent and country and among every race on earth, this action has been done, in every conceivable human circumstance, for every conceivable human need from

infancy and before it to extreme old age and after it, from the pinnacles of earthly greatness to the refuge of fugitives in the caves and dens of the earth. Men have found no better thing than this to do for kings in their crowning and for criminals going to the scaffold; for armies in triumph or for a bride and bridegroom in a little country church; for the proclamation of a dogma or for a good crop of wheat; for the wisdom of the Parliament of a mighty nation or for a sick old woman afraid to die; for a schoolboy sitting an examination or for Columbus setting out to discover America;...because the Turk was at the gates of Vienna...[and] on the beach at Dunkirk;...tremulously, by an old monk on the fiftieth anniversary of his vows; furtively, by an exiled bishop who had hewn timber all day in a prison camp near Murmansk; gorgeously, for the canonisation of S. Joan of Arc.... And best of all, week by week and month by month, on a hundred thousand successive Sundays, faithfully, unfailingly, across all the parishes of christendom, the pastors have done this just to *make* the holy common people of God.[2]

Yes indeed, it is the Mass, the Eucharist, that "makes" the Catholic people of God, shapes a community of Christ as nothing else Catholic can—neither letter nor law, neither catechism nor creed. Here the risen Christ is gloriously present as two or three of you, two or three thousand of you, gather together in his name. Here Christ himself speaks to you when Old and New Testaments are proclaimed to you—when the Lord tells Abraham to leave his country and kindred for a land he knows not where, and Micah tells God's people that what the Lord requires of them is justice; when teenage Mary responds through an angel, "Whatever you want, Lord," and Paul tells you that he knows nothing save Christ and him crucified. Here Christ rests on your hand and on your tongue, makes your body a temple of God as truly as is the tabernacle. Here Jesus says to you, "This is my body [and it is] given for you" (Lk 22:19). Here is the Bread of Life—a food that paradoxically is not changed into us; we are changed into Christ. Here each Sunday the recessional sends you back into the world to feed the hungry and slake the thirsty, to clothe the naked and welcome the stranger, to visit the lonely on a hospital bed or behind bars.

Here, in the Eucharistic liturgy, you and I re-present the most remarkable love history has ever experienced, the love that persuaded God's only Son to wear our flesh, to walk our earth, to die in our stead, to leave with us his body and blood, his soul and his very Godhead. Here, in this Eucharist that literally translates as "thanksgiving," you and I make our return of love, do what Jesus asked "in memory" of him. Here is, or should be, the center of our spiritual life, the core of our devotion. Here, as nowhere else, we bend our whole being before the Lord and sing with St. Thomas Aquinas:

> Godhead here in hiding, whom I do adore
> Masked by these bare shadows, shape and nothing more:
> See, Lord, at thy service low lies here a heart
> Lost, all lost in wonder at the God thou art.[3]

II

It is in this context, the Eucharist, that the organ you bless fulfils its highest purpose. Indeed you can, and probably will, utilize it for recitals other than Eucharistic. But, as Archbishop Keeler phrased it so pithily, "The organ has been installed so that the celebration of the liturgy may become more beautiful and solemn." This raises some critical questions about our "new song to the Lord." Let me share with you what I, hardly a musician, have discovered late in life about the intimate link between music and the Mass, between song and the Sacrifice, between lyrics and liturgy. I want simply to say that music is power, music is worship, music is community.[4]

First, music is power. Whether it's vocal or instrumental, the blues or ballet, folk music or chamber, jazz or opera, rock or country, guitar or organ, music rivals economics and love in its power to make the world go round. Power? This past Memorial Day 250,000 folk of all ages on the Capitol Lawn thrilled to the voices of Judy Collins and Mac Davis, Gladys Knight and the Boys Choir of Harlem, to the National Symphony Orchestra. Your children are charmed each Christmas by *Nutcracker*, and your teenagers rock to Bob Dylan and Carly Simon, to The Who and The Carpenters, to Red Hot Chili Peppers. Hard rock, for good or ill, is shaping the sex life of countless teenagers. Your own feet start itching when you hear a Strauss waltz; your heart beats faster to the rhythms of "America the Beautiful" or Sousa's "The Stars and Stripes Forever." Beethoven's "Ode to Joy" sends newlyweds out of church in ecstasy. I write my most effective homilies with Chopin or George Winston or Tchaikovsky as background. And what was it that for decades powered the African-American powerless in their struggle for human living? The unforgettable chant "We shall overcome."

Second, music is worship. Our Catholic liturgy labors under a heavy burden. Not only is there a whole book entitled *Why Catholics Can't Sing;* uncounted Catholics see song at Mass as at best part of the *décor*, on a par with the stained-glass windows or the flowers at the feet of our Lady. The Catholic reality is quite different: Music is liturgy. You are entitled to disbelieve a visiting Jesuit; you cannot shrug off the Second Vatican Council: "Sacred music united to words...forms a necessary or integral part of the solemn liturgy."[5] And "In the Latin Church the pipe organ is to be held in high esteem, for it...adds a wondrous splendor to the Church's ceremonies and powerfully lifts minds up to God and to heavenly things."[6]

Why music in the liturgy? Because music keeps our worship from lapsing into a sheer "head trip," naked words that lift to God nothing but our intellect, our ability to form concepts, to make judgments. Sing, and the whole man, the whole woman, comes to life—voice box, diaphragm, stomach muscles, yes your emotions, your feelings, so much in you that begs mutely to be let loose, to shake the Spirit loose.

You see, worship is very much like love; in fact, genuine worship is an expression of love. If that is true, then the more of myself that goes into my worship, the more perfectly I worship. What was Jesus' first commandment? Love God not only "with all your soul and all your mind," but "with all your heart" (Mt 22:37).[7] You can murmur "Silent Night, Holy Night" till the cows come home, but it is only when you sing it, or let the organ music roll over you, that the goose pimples tingle and you feel the pull of Bethlehem. I know, very few of our voices will ever make Pavarotti envious; my own singing has put many a musician's teeth on edge; but that is not the point. We worship not only in spirit and in truth but with our full Catholic humanity when as a community we "sing a new song to the Lord," when our community lifts its combined voice, its heart, to God.

Our community. Music is community. Remember, the Eucharist is not a private party, a thousand individuals praying to God in isolation. Good liturgy is done by community, in community, for community. Why? Simply because the Eucharist is St. Paul's "one body," where no one can say to any other, "I have no need of you" (1 Cor 12:20-21).

Precisely here music plays a superlative part; for liturgical music is done by community, in community, for community. Each of us contributes. Within the same notes there are overtones and undertones. You have to follow a beat, the pulse or throb of measured music—up and down, loud and soft. Speak the Lord's Prayer and it really doesn't matter how you say it. Sing the Lord's Prayer and you're part of a distinctive whole: hundreds of voices, now light as silk, now heavy as metal, now praising God's kingdom, now bending to God's will, now pleading for bread, now begging for forgiveness and escape from the Evil One.

III

A final word, quite personal. This celebration—of your 125-year-old parish and your new organ—will conclude with a short prayer by your archbishop. I hope and pray that you will not let it pass over you lightly; for it contains an important monosyllable. The prayer will run: "The Lord is worthy of all praise. May He give you the gift of striving to sing a new song to Him with your voices, your hearts, and your lives, so that one day you may sing that song forever in heaven."

Sing a new song with your *lives*. The song that erupts from our voice box is not an end in itself. The vocal song should be a symbol—symbol of the song that is my life. Does my life sing, to God and my sisters and brothers, the songs that burst from my lips? Concretely, does my Christian joy hymn to those around me that "Christ the Lord is risen today"? Does my catholicity, my love for all God's children, sing that "in Christ there is no East or West,/in him no South or North,/ but one great fellowship of love/throughout the whole wide earth"? Does my living hope sing that "the Lord is my shepherd,/there is nothing I shall want"? Does my church life sing that "the Church's one foundation is Jesus Christ her Lord"? A fruitful meditation for every Christian: Is it my *life* that is singing "a new song to the Lord"?

Good friends in Christ: This anniversary year, indeed this very afternoon, is one of those blessed opportunities God gives us for a movement that should be part and parcel of our lives. I mean... conversion. Literally, conversion means a turning. In our Christian case, not always or usually a turning *from*...from serious sin, from raging infidelity. More often, a turning *to*...a fresh turning to Christ, to the downtrodden images of Christ, a more profound fidelity, a richer fulness to our Christian existence, a more exuberant joy in what we believe and how we worship. It is in this sense that we should be singing a *new* song to the Lord. One question: Are we?

Shrine of the Sacred Heart
Baltimore, Maryland
June 13, 1993

31
LOVE HEALS
Homily 1 for a Medical School Graduation

- Isaiah 61:1-3
- Romans 12:9-21
- Matthew 5:13-16

Twenty-four hundred years ago, a friend of yours named Hippocrates used to say he would rather know what sort of person has a disease than what sort of disease a person has.[1] It fits beautifully with his aphorism, "Where you find love of the human person, there you find love of the Art."[2] It harmonizes neatly with a powerful two-word declaration I discovered in Dr. Bernie Siegel: "Love heals."[3] Therefore what? Therefore my homily.[4]

Not surprisingly, three movements to my song and dance: (1) the world you are entering; (2) your calling within that world; (3) a personal plea.

I

First, the world you are entering—the world you have already entered. Your world. In the area of health, that world is a paradox, if not a contradiction.[5] A world where over a billion people live in poverty, over two billion lack safe sanitation, 100 million have no shelter whatsoever. A world where a quarter million of its children are dying every week, where this decade alone perhaps 150 million children will die, mostly from diseases we have learned to cure. A world where more than a million girls die each year simply because they are born female, where 500,000 women die in childbirth every year, where about 150,000 pregnancies end in abortion every day. A world where 36 million men, women, and children eke out life as refugees—that cold abstraction "displaced persons." A world where the longer humans live, the more of a problem they are for society.

Look at our own dear "land of the free." An America where the infant mortality rate is higher than that of 19 other industrialized nations. An America where in 1990 407,000 minors were placed in foster homes. An America where each day at least three children die of injuries afflicted by abusive parents. An America where each day over 500 children 10 to 14 begin using illegal drugs, over a thousand start on alcohol. An America where one child in eight has an alcoholic parent. An America where each day over 1400 teenage girls become mothers—two thirds of them unmarried. An America where among teens 15 to 19 the third-leading cause of death is firearms.[6] An America whose capital city starts school with a weapons check. An America where the rate of teenage suicide has tripled in 30 years, where a million youngsters sleep on our streets each night. An America where "The epidemic of HIV infection is a *national* disaster,"[7] where, as *Fortune* magazine put it, "AIDS has turned youthful experimentation with sex into Russian roulette."[8] An America where poverty breeds violence, sexual abuse, hopelessness.

It is an America where one of every four youngsters you see is living in some sort of hell.

II

This world, this America, leads into my second point: your calling within that context. As Mario Cuomo has insisted, "illness does not occur in a vacuum,...the roots of illness are usually deeply implanted in homelessness, in poverty, in other persistent social ills"[9]—joblessness, substandard housing, illicit drugs. He went on to write:

> Health, perhaps more than any other aspect of our lives, depends upon the innerconnectedness of everything else we are and do. The very word "health" has the same root as "whole." It denotes an integrity based upon the immensely complex synergy that includes the workings of the human body and all the external forces that affect it. Health is not given, nor taken away, in a vacuum.... [T]he relationship between illness...and poverty...is not just a grotesque coincidence. It is causal. It is real. It is historic.[10]

But, good doctors all, if illness does not occur in a vacuum, then your treatment of illness dare not occur in a vacuum. Whether administrator or surgeon, internist or nurse, radiologist or anesthesiologist, you will not lead our church or our country into the 21st century if you operate with a tunnel vision, if your administrative ability is bounded by red ink and black, if your surgery reveals simply a superb artist or a journeyman mechanic, if your eyes cannot see beyond the immediate cause of malnutrition or a gunshot wound, a smoke-blackened lung or an intestinal inflammation, high blood pressure or rheumatoid arthritis. I submit that your God-given vocation goes beyond your ability to cure. It extends to your power to heal. Let me explain.

Over the years I have made three significant discoveries. (1) I cannot understand my country today if I do not know where America came from and where it's been. (2) I cannot understand my church today if I do not know where Catholicism came from and where it's been. (3) I cannot understand who I am if I do not know where this complex, paradoxical creature came from and where I've been. May I suggest that the healthcare leaders of the future will be the men and women who are concerned to discover where their patients come from and where they've been? Not only their medical history on a reception-room questionnaire; their broader experience of human and inhuman living—their integral humanity.

There is something supremely Catholic about this. For in the Catholic vision of sickness you are privileged to touch, as truly as a priest is privileged to touch, a human person, an image of God, a man or woman at a critical moment in human living: when he or she is working out his or her salvation. When Christian hope is threatened by fear; when the sufferer can feel as forsaken as Jesus was on his cross; when life or death stands at a bedside in a white coat. When a child of God is begging mutely to be treated not as a wrist tag but as a person.

This raises a neuralgic question: What sort of medicine man/ medicine woman does such a situation demand? For in Catholic social thought, professions are not simply interest groups or trade associations; they bear special social responsibilities. Yours is the primary community that must respond to the right to healthcare. And the Catholic vision calls for special people. It demands a man or woman intensely aware of a vocation. A Christian vocation. It is the mission of Jesus, who came not to be served but to serve. It is a mission that falls under the second great commandment of the gospel: You must love your sisters and brothers like other selves.

I know, the word "love" is bandied like a yo-yo, is used of everything from a half century of husband-and-wife caring, through a one-night stand after a singles' bar pickup, to TV's gross "Game of Love." To bring your love down to Christian earth, mull over the first two passages you have plucked from God's own Book. The passage from Isaiah speaks plainly to you: The Spirit of the Lord has sent you "to bind up the brokenhearted, to comfort [those] who mourn" (Isa 61:1-2). Not only to bind up broken bodies; broken hearts as well. And

St. Paul urges you to "let [your] love be genuine," to "weep with those who weep" (Rom 12:9, 15).

What does the Spirit of the Lord, what does "genuine love," demand of you? This coming year your class will invade 31 States, DC, and Honolulu. Like it or not, aware of it or not, you will put a stamp on that little acre of God's world, because you will touch x-number of persons, more or less alive, not only with your stethoscope or scalpel but with your total self. For good or ill, for good health or bad, each of you will touch thousands of bodies—more importantly perhaps, can touch thousands of hearts. I suggest that the form of love which comes closest to your vocation, the form of love that takes little of your medical time and enriches your medical lore, is...compassion. Not pity, which looks down from a superior posture. Rather the compassion that formed the stuff of God-in-flesh, that made him totally happy only when he was looking with love into the eyes of a sinful or suffering man or woman.

Here I presume to repeat the paragraph I quoted to you at the outset of your GU medical career, a passage from Dr. Richard Selzer's personal experience, a passage I hope you have matured into during these four years:

> A surgeon does not slip from his mother's womb with compassion smeared upon him like the drippings of his birth. It is much later that it comes. No easy shaft of grace this, but the cumulative murmuring of the numberless wounds he has dressed, the incisions he has made, all the sores and ulcers and cavities he has touched in order to heal. In the beginning it is barely audible, a whisper, as from many mouths. Slowly it gathers, rising from the streaming flesh until, at last, it is a pure *calling*—an exclusive sound, like the cry of certain solitary birds—telling that out of the resonance between the sick man and the one who tends him there may spring that profound courtesy that the religious call Love.[11]

But the love is not all on your side. Let me ask you to ponder, and respond to, a sentence from Dr. Siegel: "I am convinced that unconditional love is the most powerful known stimulant of the immune system." Unconditional love within the suffering man or woman, yes, but a love stimulated by a doctor who "can teach them to love themselves and others fully."[12] I am impressed by a story Dr. Siegel relates. Sara comes to him with breast cancer, but also smoking. Sheepishly she says, "I suppose you're going to tell me to stop smoking." "No," he says, "I'm going to tell you to love yourself. Then you'll stop."[13] Are you actually infringing on the psychiatrist's couch if you advise your patients to love themselves? Will you ever touch them with other than professional hands? Can you somehow give even one of them a sense of worth, a reason for living, a meaning to dying? Or will you echo the agonizing admission of a professor at Boston University's School of Medicine: "we more or less abandon dying patients. When there is nothing more medicine can offer, we turn them over to the nursing staff, and we don't see them anymore"?[14] Will you leave it to Mother Teresa to hold the AIDS-afflicted in caring arms? Or to Jack Kevorkian?[15]

In brief, can you subscribe to, can you live, the vision of tomorrow's medicine as Jewish Dr. Siegel has already experienced it? In his provocative book *Love, Medicine & Miracles* he declares apodictically: "Remember I said love *heals*. I do not claim love *cures* everything but it can *heal* and in the process of healing cures occur also."[16]

III

This leads directly to my third point: a personal plea. Tomorrow is...Pentecost. Your special celebration. For Pentecost is mission, a sending. Not only of the original apostles—Peter and Andrew, James and John. You too are sent. Not only by Georgetown; by God as well. To do what? Your choice of a Gospel tells you what: to be salt and light.

Salt your acre of the earth, do in your profession, for your people, what salt did for meat and fish in early Palestine: preserve, keep from spoiling, from rotting. Not just the flesh; the human person coming apart. Even more broadly, salt the inhuman and immoral structures of your universe. Change a society that misshapes God's images through hunger and homelessness, joblessness and hopelessness, casual sex and violence, coke and alcohol, and shunts them to your hospitals and mental institutions, your jails and homes for the unproductive elderly, and expects of you medical miracles, challenges you to raise them from the dead. You must cry to heaven and to earth against societal systems that wheel into your wards inhuman beings whom society has rejected, men, women, and yes children whose bones and blood, whose hearts and hopes, are beyond repairing. Cry out against this, for your tongues as well as your lives must echo the declaration of a justice of the New York State Supreme Court: "A society that loses its sense of outrage is doomed to extinction."[17]

Be light to your world. Not just penetrating diagnoses and insightful prognoses. Even more importantly, shed the healing power of your whole person, your competence and compassion, over the community in which you live and move and have your being. More broadly still, make sure with your corporate influence that the Catholic vision of healthcare reform reaches clearly and persuasively the ears of Hillary Rodham Clinton. For if it does not, you ministers of wholeness will not merely suffer a political defeat. Access to healthcare may indeed reach all; but countless men, women, and children who are *cured* will still yearn fruitlessly to be *healed*.

Graduates dear to my heart: Throughout this Eucharist that is literally translated "thanksgiving," my prayer for you rests in three verbs that are simple but glowingly warm: God lead you, God feed you, God speed you.

Holy Trinity Church
Washington, D.C.
May 29, 1993

32

BE COMPASSIONATE....
Homily 2 for a Medical School Graduation

• Philippians 4:4-9
• Luke 6:36-38

"Be compassionate..." (Lk 6:36). A remarkably pertinent command your class[1] has lifted from the lips of Jesus. Pertinent because compassion is a quality associated with the medical profession since the heyday of Hippocrates. I celebrate your selection, but I wonder. I wonder if the classroom and the gurney have left you time to contemplate that biblical text: how profound, how perilous, and how personal it is. Profound because of what Jesus adds; perilous because of the social context that surrounds your vocation; personal because the words are spoken to you. So then, three stages to my song and dance: Jesus, context, you.

I

First, Jesus. You see, Jesus did not stop with the brief injunction "Be compassionate." He told us how profound our compassion must be, to what heights it must rise. "Be compassionate, just as your Father is compassionate" (Lk 6:36). Be compassionate the way God is compassionate. But can this be for real? What does it mean to say God is compassionate? Not to bog down in intellectual smoke, take a swift look at what God has *done*. If you want to touch the compassion of God, look at God's unique Son. Look at Jesus.

You see, in Jesus God's compassion took flesh. For if compassion means not a weak, embarrassed sympathy but a fellowship in feeling; if to be compassionate is literally to "suffer with" another; if compassion asks us to go where it hurts, to enter into places of pain, to share in brokenness and confusion, fear and anguish; if compassion challenges

155

us to cry out with those in misery, to mourn with those who are lonely, to weep with those in tears[2]—then go back 2000 years to a crib and a cross.

Look at a contradiction only a superimaginative God could have invented. I mean a God-man conceived in a Jewish teenager's womb, born in a feeding trough for animals, fleeing to Egypt a refugee from a frightened king. I mean God's Son touching blind eyes to sight, touching leprous skin to health, touching a widow's dead son to life. I mean God's Son experiencing what we experience as we experience it: sweating as we sweat, hungering as we hunger, tiring as we tire, hearing his relatives shout he is mad, weeping over his city Jerusalem and his friend Lazarus. I mean God's Son sold for silver, mocked for a fool, lashed with whips, crowned with thorns, pinned to twin beams of wood. An early Christian hymn reproduced by St. Paul encapsulated all this:

> Christ Jesus,
> though he was in the form of God,
> did not count equality with God
> a thing to be clutched,
> but emptied himself of it,
> to take on the form of a slave
> and become like men and women.
> And having assumed human form,
> he still further humbled himself
> with an obedience that meant death,
> even death on a cross.
>
> (Phil 2:5-8)

And why? The evangelist John summed it up swiftly: "God so loved the world that He gave His only Son" (Jn 3:16). Paul put it poignantly, phrased it even more personally: The Son of God "loved *me* and gave himself for *me*" (Gal 2:20). Compassion is a synonym for love. And if, as John said, "God is love" (1 Jn 4:16), then God is compassion. Not only *has* compassion; God *is* compassion.

II

Second, your social context. This is what makes compassion perilous, puts compassion at risk. Bluntly, can you afford to be compassionate? Here two contemporary settings are particularly pertinent. One stems from politics, the other from economics.

From politics. Some years ago an uncommonly caring Senator,

the late Hubert Humphrey, was questioned about compassion in politics. Senator Humphrey picked up a long pencil with a small eraser at the end and said:

> Gentlemen, look at this pencil. Just as the eraser is only a very small part of this pencil and is used only when you make a mistake, so compassion is only called upon when things get out of hand. The main part of life is competition, only the eraser is compassion. It is sad to say, gentlemen, but in politics compassion is just part of the competition.[3]

From economics. Economics is not my long suit, but as I read the literature on healthcare to come, my compassion for you rises to new heights. Simply, I want state-of-the-art treatment for all who ail, but in grim reality your care must be rationed.

Last year, on a plane from San Francisco to Baltimore, I sat next to the then president of the American Urological Association. Our conversation centered on his forthcoming presidential address to the association. In the course of his actual address, he quoted with approval a bioethicist I had commended to him: "Health care is not the only social good—it enjoys no automatic claim to take precedence over other essential goods." He went on to say:

> Our society is confronted with an economic reality. It is no longer capable of supporting all its social wants. It is now confronted with the painful and unpleasant obligation of establishing priorities. Public health care spending must be assigned its proper place among other social goods such as education, drug programs, public transportation, rescue of our inner-cities, national defense and especially the preservation of our nation's international competitiveness and, thus, our national economy. Our standard of living, including our health care delivery system, is based on the strength of that economy. We cannot "wound the goose who's laying the golden eggs."[4]

Two social realities: (1) a widespread conviction that compassion must yield to the more compelling reality of competition; (2) an economic situation that compels compassion to yield to grim financial realism.

III

These social realities lead rigorously into my third point, the personal aspect: compassion and you. Caught between the compassion of Jesus in the first century and the harsh realities of living and dying in the 20th, what to do?

1) For your sanity and your sanctity, I suggest you do what Jesus did: retire. Not permanently. Retire on occasion to the shore of the sea or the top of a mountain or even the harshness of a desert. Why? Like Jesus, to be alone with your God. Not that God is absent from the OR; only that God can be lost in the bones and the blood, in the mucus and the metastasis. Not to escape reality; simply to interrupt the ordinary pattern of your existence; to see more clearly. See what? See what a sacred but exhausting profession might be doing to your life, to your relationships—with patients, with friends, with family, with God. To mull over the suicides that plague your profession. To see whether healing has made you more human or less, more divine or less. To refill the cup—the cup of compassion.

For compassion does not come out of a test tube, from a prescription, from a medical text. Like the love that is its synonym, compassion can be defined in a classroom, but it cannot be taught. It is a gift—a gift that comes if we are open to others, to the crucified images of Christ. A gift that is given especially if we are open to God. For the compassion of a Christian is not simply a natural reaction to suffering— to a child starving in the sub-Sahara, a mother raped in Bosnia, a Jacqueline Kennedy Onassis leveled by lymphoma. The compassion of Christ is a God-given gift, a gift God gives to all who yearn for it, who beg for it, who suffer for it. And compassion can die, ravaged by routine, worn away with worry, deadened by defeat. The cup must be refilled.

2) From such reflection a significant realization may emerge: Compassion is not a thoughtless thing, sheer recklessness. It is not weeping with a scalpel in your hand. My friends among Dominican theologians would counsel prudence in its best sense: not cowardice, simply putting reason into virtue. None of you, not all of you, not the whole of your profession can touch all the needs of an ailing world that cries out to you. You will have to choose whom to treat, decide how much or how little you can do, perhaps at times utter a sorrowful no in the face of 37 million uninsured. But those you do choose, those to whom you say yes, lay on you a heavy burden, a high privilege. For each comes to you as a person, an unrepeatable person. And each comes to you...afraid. Oh yes, they come to you in hope, because of your competence. But what they need is something more than sheer skill. It is summed up in the First Letter of John: "Perfect love casts out fear" (1 Jn 4:18). They need a physician who cares. You may not be able to cure my body, but you have a tremendous power: to heal my spirit, to heal my fear.

Last week I read a fascinating fact: "insurance companies have found that if a wife kisses her husband good-bye in the morning he has fewer auto accidents and lives five years longer."[5] This is not my prescription for the medical profession; I do say that love, caring, compassion should play as large a role in the life of a physician as it plays in the life of a priest.

3) Finally, to take compassion out of a welter of words, to allow compassion to take wing, let me share an insight I delight to recall. It stems from an imaginative Presbyterian preacher and novelist. He claimed that the religious man or woman is "a queer mixture" of three persons: "the poet, the lunatic, the lover."[6] As you move on to your next level in the art of healing, that insight compels from me a corresponding three-tiered prayer. I pray that the poet may always find a place in you; for the poet is a person of profound faith, seeing with new eyes, seeing beneath the surface of things—in your case, seeing in each suffering human who seeks your healing not primarily a patient, a wrist tag, but an image of the crucified Christ, a vulnerable human mutely begging, if not for a cure from your skill, at least for some measure of healing from your caring. I pray that there may ever be a fair measure of lunacy in you: what St. Paul called the foolishness of the cross, the idiocy of self-sacrifice, perhaps the mad exchange of all else for God and those you serve; for herein lies your Christian hope. And I pray that, however radical the risk, however costly your own cross, on that cross you will always be Christ the lover, arms extended to your little world not only for its physical well-being but for its growth in faith, in hope, in love.

Why all this? Because precisely here—as poet, lunatic, and lover— lies your own growth into Christ. Precisely here lies your own healing. Precisely here you may, with God's rich grace, realize the proverb Jesus put on the lips of his cynical townspeople: "Doctor, heal yourself!" (Lk 4:23).

Holy Trinity Church
Washington, D.C.
May 28, 1994

33

CALL MY TRUE LOVE TO MY DANCE
Sermon for a Christmas Chorale

- Luke 2:1-20
- Matthew 2:1-12

Good friends: Unknowingly, your songsters have done more than simply sing like angels. Three of the pieces you have just heard have stimulated the three stages of my own song and dance, the three points I shall develop succinctly in these "Reflections on the Season."[1] I mean (1) "O magnum mysterium," (2) "Hodie Christus natus est," and (3) "Tomorrow Shall Be My Dancing Day." In swift succession they sing of yesterday, today, and tomorrow. And so shall I.

I

First, yesterday, "O magnum mysterium," "O Magnificent Mystery." For Christians, Christmas will always be wound about with... wonder. Oh, not wonder as uncertainty, puzzlement, perplexity: I wonder if there will ever be permanent peace between the PLO and Israel; I wonder if bombs will ever cease blasting Bosnia; I wonder if our Congress will ever again capture the confidence of our people. No. Christmas is wonder because Christmas is awe, amazement, delight, surprise. Awe because our very God touches our earth in person, in our flesh, in a feeding trough for animals. Amazement because "angels we have heard on high," God's messengers proclaiming peace to God's friends. Delight as we spy shepherds hastening over hills to greet a long-sought Savior. Surprise that a star should send astrologers from the East to lay gold, frankincense, and myrrh before "omnipotence in bonds."

The wonder of it never pales. But in the midst of all this, most awesome and amazing, incomparably delightful and surprising, is the literal *littleness* of it all. As we Christians see it, Jesus could have entered our earth full-grown, could have stridden the dust of Palestine with the strength of a Schwarzenegger, could have put a hammer lock on Herod in his protected palace. He could have come unburdened by the vulnerability of all that is human.

He could have, but he did not. Jesus came to us as a child, a newborn infant. The most vulnerable of humans. To stand before Bethlehem's manger is to stand before mystery. If we Christians are not horribly mistaken, God's unique Son wanted to experience what we experience as we experience it. Not only dying as we die, but born as we are born: born of a Jewish teenager in a forgotten corner of God's good earth. What he knew as Son of God, he wanted to see, hear, touch, taste, and smell as Son of man. Yes, even feed at his mother's breast. A hard saying indeed. Little wonder that in the fifth century the Christian patriarch of Constantinople, a powerful prelate named Nestorius, proclaimed in protest: "Does God have a mother? [He does not.]" "It is not right to say of God that He sucked milk...." "A born God, a dead God, a buried God I cannot adore."[2]

Why did Jesus want to experience all this? Ultimately, the reason lies deep in the mystery that is God. But it was Jesus himself who broke the secret to a Pharisee named Nicodemus: "God so loved the world..." (Jn 3:16).

We are indeed bent low before mystery—mystery that understandably makes no sense to such as do not share our faith. Still, for our purposes this afternoon, it is enough that all of us can focus with reverence on the child of a Jewish mother, a child who would grow up to shed his blood for all of us who rejoice to be children of Abraham.

II

This leads directly to my second stage, our second song, "Hodie Christus natus est," "Today Christ Is Born." Today. You see, for all its uniqueness, Bethlehem is not an isolated experience. God's Son took flesh in Christ to create other Christs. What Christians should see in each Christmas crib, what others may see without doing violence to their convictions, is not simply the original Jesus but every child born of God's love.

It isn't easy. All you have to do is thumb through the 1994 Report of the Children's Defense Fund on the Costs of Child Poverty. The title of the volume is itself sobering: *Wasting America's Future.*[3] Despite advances in childcare, the fresh figures are depressing, continue to confound us. One in five American children is poor, 14.6 million. The younger children are, the poorer they are. Nor does it stop there. "Child poverty stalks its survivors down every avenue of their lives."[4] It puts them at terrible risk. They are far more likely than you and I to live hungry and homeless, to be sick in mind and body, to be uneducated, to be teen parents, to have an abnormal adolescence. Poverty even kills. Low-income children are two times more likely to die from birth defects, three times more likely to die from all causes combined, four times more likely to die in fires, five times more likely to die from infectious diseases and parasites, six times more likely to die from other diseases.[5]

A sermon is not the place to argue about causes. Does child poverty go back to the welfare system, to teenage pregnancy, to irresponsible parents? Or must some of the blame descend on "a society that guarantees [the unproductive poor] a prison bed (for over $30,000 a year) but refuses to provide them a Head Start (for less than $3,800 a year) or a summer job (for less than $1,400) to help them succeed"?[6]

My point here is quite different but not utterly unrelated. In the Judeo-Christian tradition, each of these children comes into this world a child beloved of God. When any one of these infants is born, each Christian can say, must say, "Hodie Christus natus est," "Today Christ is born." Here is the dark side of the Christmas story, the side we brush off because it tarnishes the turkey, taints the tinsel. It is for such as these that God's Son took our flesh, as much as for you and me. To remove them from the Christmas story, to people the stable with shepherds and astrologers alone, is to insist on the history at the expense of the mystery.

The history at the expense of the mystery. Each Christmas, at much personal risk, I take a fresh look at the crib. The original Christ child is no longer there; he has fled to Egypt, moved to Nazareth, grown up, been crucified, returned to his Father. What do I see? At times an infant bursting with health, crooning in joy. More often an infant left on the hospital doorstep; more often a little one with Down's syndrome, or encephalitic, or undernourished, or simply unloved. Or perhaps the crib is empty because a child was forcibly kept from ever resting there.

III

But lest I strip all the tinsel from your holiday, lest I sound like Scrooge, a third stage: tomorrow. I mean your carol "Tomorrow Shall Be My Dancing Day." You see, tomorrow spells hope. Two feasts beckon this coming week: for Christians, Christmas, a child who brought new life to a dying world, by dying restored our life; for the Jewish people, Chanukah (Hanukkah), the Feast of Lights or of Dedication, a purified temple and a small cruse of oil that refused to die, that lit their holy lamps for eight days. Despite all the past that divides us, the eight days of Chanukah and the 12 days of Christmas have something significant in common, significant for our relationship and for our children: In both feasts gifts are exchanged and contributions are made to the poor. Why significant? A short story told by a rabbi is particularly provocative.

A man had been wandering about in a forest for several days unable to find his way out. Seeing another man approaching, he asked him, "Brother, will you please tell me the way out of the forest?" Said the other, "I don't know the way out either, for I too have been wandering here for many days. But this much I can tell you: The way I have gone is not the way."[7]

And so with us. The separate ways we have been going, we two covenanted peoples, these ways are not *the* way. Somehow we must join hands and look for the way together. Two small beginnings. Remember, in both communities gifts are exchanged and contributions are made to the poor. But the gifts we exchange dare not be segregated, kept separate within each community. Before all else, the gift we exchange must be a love that alone can keep us from living forever in hostility, in a tenuous truce. Then it is that we can join hands in giving ourselves together to the children whose lives are living deaths. If the Child of Bethlehem still keeps us at arm's length, perhaps the children of God's predilection, the living dead, will provide a fresh start through our tragic brokenness.

A paradox indeed, but a paradox with hope: hope for our broken children, hope for our broken communities. A dream? Yes. Farfetched? Not really. With God all things are possible. So then, dear God, this Christmas, this Chanukah, compel me to think big. Drive my imagination to run wild. Let me, in the words of the carol, "call my true love to my dance." *Our* dance.

Church of St. Aloysius Gonzaga
Washington, D.C.
December 18, 1994

NOTES

Homily 1

1. See the editorial "Children Too Ready To Die Young," *Washington Post*, Nov. 3, 1993, A26.
2. Time prevented me from adding repentance to Gospel joy, especially the extraordinary joy in heaven over a repentant sinner, as well as the joy of the prodigal's father over his son's return.
3. Sister Mary Ignatius, "Discovery," *Messenger of the Sacred Heart* 77, no. 2 (February 1942) 58.

Homily 2

1. Actually, it is only after the Magi leave Jerusalem that the star clearly functions as a guide for them, specifying where precisely the child was (Mt 2:9). See Daniel J. Harrington, S.J., *The Gospel of Matthew* (Sacra pagina 1; Collegeville, Minn.: Liturgical, 1991) 42 and 43.
2. See Harrington, ibid. 47: "The historicity of these episodes [Mt 2] remains an open question that probably can never be definitively decided. The more important issue is determining what these stories meant to Matthew and his community." Harrington gives a swift summary of arguments pro and con (ibid.).
3. Harrington (ibid. 43) reminds us that "Despite popular tradition, it is not necessary to read Luke 2:7 as referring to a cave or stable. It is more likely a reference to the part of a private house set apart for animals that could be used also as guest quarters in an emergency situation. So there is no need to see a direct contradiction between Matthew and Luke on this point. Both may well have envisioned Mary, Joseph, and Jesus in a house."

4. The focus of this third point stems from the actual context of the homily. It was delivered during a five-day retreat/workshop for priests of the Diocese of Erie, Pa., within my project Preaching the Just Word, an effort to move the *preaching* of social-justice issues more effectively into all the pulpits and congregations of our country.

5. Louis S. Richman, "Struggling To Save Our Kids," in a Special Report in *Fortune* 126, no. 3 (Aug. 10, 1992) 34-40, at 34.

6. See ibid. 35-36.

7. Introduction to Kevin Casey, *Children of Eve* (New York: Covenant House, 1991) iii.

Homily 3

1. See Joseph A. Fitzmyer, S.J., *The Gospel according to Luke (X-XXIV)* (Garden City, N.Y.: Doubleday, 1985) 1503.

2. I have this story from the sermon of a Protestant preacher, who heard it from a woman doctor from Mafraq, over coffee in the Beirut Intercontinental Hotel. I have shortened the story somewhat, without omitting essentials.

Homily 4

1. Joseph A. Fitzmyer, S.J., *The Gospel according to Luke (X-XXIV)* (Garden City, N.Y.: Doubleday, 1985) 1508.

2. St. Ambrose, *Exposition of the Gospel according to Luke* 10.121 (Corpus christianorum lat. 14, 379).

3. See Fitzmyer (n. 1 above) 1510.

4. Graham Greene, *Monsignor Quixote* (New York: Simon and Schuster, 1982) 69-70.

Homily 5

1. See John L. McKenzie, S.J., "Widow," *Dictionary of the Bible* (New York: Macmillan, 1965) 927.

2. On symbol see Avery Dulles, S.J., "The Symbolic Structure of Revelation," *Theological Studies* 41 (1980) 51-73, esp. 55-56.

3. I am aware that some Scripture scholars, e.g. Raymond Brown, translate the Greek *ide* as "Here is" rather than "Look!" No problem; I simply find the more literal translation more practical, more vivid, for preaching. I am aware that the New Revised Standard Version combines the two in Jn 1:36: "Look, here is the Lamb of God!"

4. See Raymond E. Brown, S.S., *The Gospel according to John (i-xii)* (Garden City, N.Y.: Doubleday, 1966) 58.

5. See Raymond E. Brown, S.S., *The Gospel according to John (xiii-xxi)* (Garden City, N.Y.: Doubleday, 1970) 907.

6. Ibid. 926.

7.   Elizabeth A. Johnson, C.S.J., "Mary and the Female Face of God," *Theological Studies* 50 (1989) 500-526, at 520.

8.   *Osservatore romano*, Sept. 21, 1978, 2.

9.   Henri de Lubac, S.J., "Meditation on the Church," in *Vatican II: An Interfaith Appraisal*, ed. John H. Miller, C.S.C. (Notre Dame, Ind.: University of Notre Dame, 1966) 258-66, at 259 and 261.

Homily 7

1.   Or possibly the diluted, vinegary wine that was actually given him, a wine drunk by soldiers and laborers to quench their thirst (see ibid. 909).

2.   See Raymond E. Brown, S.S., *The Gospel according to John (xiii-xxi)* (Garden City, N.Y.: Doubleday, 1970) 908-9, 927-30.

3.   From Patrice J. Tuohy's interview with Thea Bowman, as reproduced in *Sister Thea Bowman, Shooting Star: Selected Writings and Speeches*, ed. Celestine Cepress, FSPA (Winona, Minn.: Saint Mary's Press, 1993) 127. The interview originally appeared in *U.S. Catholic*, June 1990, 21-26.

Homily 8

1.   See Joseph A. Fitzmyer, S.J., *Paul and His Theology: A Brief Sketch* (2nd ed.; Englewood Cliffs, N.J.: Prentice-Hall, 1989) 59-60.

2.   Frederick Buechner, *The Hungering Dark* (New York: Seabury, 1969) 45-46.

Homily 9

1.   I am aware that only Luke transmits these words (23:46) as Jesus' "final words." Mt 27:46 and Mk 15:34 have "My God, my God, why have you forsaken me?" Jn 19:30 has "It is finished."

2.   See Joseph A. Fitzmyer, S.J., *The Gospel according to Luke (X-XXIV)* (Garden City, N.Y.: Doubleday, 1985) 1519.

3.   Here I have been profoundly influenced by an article written by German theologian Karl Rahner during his last years, when he was focusing ever more intensely on the cross erected over history: "Following the Crucified," *Theological Investigations* 18: *God and Revelation* (New York: Crossroad, 1983) 157-70.

4.   Ibid. 165-66.

5.   Ibid. 168.

6.   Ibid. 169.

7.   For interpretation of this passage, see Raymond E. Brown, S.S., *The Gospel according to John (i-xii)* (Garden City, N.Y.: Doubleday, 1966) 425. I favor the interpretation Brown finds more convincing: "The believer, if he dies physically, will live spiritually [v. 25]. The believer who is alive spiritually will never die spiritually [v. 26]."

Homily 10

1. The occasion for this homily was a retreat/workshop in my project Preaching the Just Word, an effort to move the preaching of social-justice issues more effectively into all the Catholic pulpits and congregations of the country.
2. Pastoral Constitution on the Church in the Modern World, no. 35.
3. *Wichita Eagle,* Jan. 30, 1994, 14A.
4. John Paul II, encyclical letter of Dec. 30, 1987 *On Social Concern,* no. 28 (tr. from the United States Catholic Conference Publication No. 205-5 [Washington, D.C.: USCC, n.d.] 48-50).

Homily 11

1. This sermon was preached at the First Presbyterian Church in Dallas, Texas, preliminary to my four addresses on Preaching the Just Word in the Brown Lecture Series, February 6-8, 1994.
2. Karl Barth, *The Epistle to the Philippians* (Nashville: John Knox, 1962) 127.
3. See the article "The Confessions of Ed Rollins," *Vanity Fair,* February 1994, 83-87, 126-28, at 128.
4. The title of the extraordinary service center operated by the community ministries of the First Presbyterian Church in Dallas.
5. 1974 Synod of Bishops, "Human Rights and Reconciliation," *Origins* 4 (1974) 318.
6. I have borrowed this from the one-page article by Joshua S. Taub, "The Face of God," *Taproot,* February 1992, 5.

Homily 12

1. Quoted in *The New Jerome Biblical Commentary,* ed. Raymond E. Brown, S.S., Joseph A. Fitzmyer, S.J., and Roland E. Murphy, O.Carm. (Englewood Cliffs, N.J.: Prentice Hall, 1990) 2:35, p. 25.
2. This homily was delivered during a five-day retreat/worship, Preaching the Just Word, for priests of the Richmond Diocese gathered in Hampton, Va.

Homily 13

1. This homily was preached during a retreat/workshop, Preaching the Just Word, primarily but not exclusively for priests and deacons of the Archdiocese of Chicago.
2. Here, as in my second point as well, I am deeply indebted to the detailed information provided by Raymond E. Brown, S.S., *The Gospel according to John (i-xii)* (Garden City, N.Y.: Doubleday, 1966) 235-50.
3. I realize that this text comes from Mark's second account of a

multiplication (8:1-9), but I am working, as does Raymond Brown (n. 2 above, 237), with "the more probable hypothesis" that this is simply another account by Mark of the multiplication in 6:30-46.

4. Vatican II, Constitution on the Sacred Liturgy, no. 10.

5. Leo XIII, *Mirae caritatis*, May 28, 1902 (Denzinger-Schönmetzer, ed. 32 [1963] 3364).

6. The ideas in this paragraph, originally borrowed from the insightful New Testament scholar David Stanley, S.J., I have developed more at length elsewhere, e.g. in my address "Characteristics of Social Justice Spirituality," *Origins* 24, no. 9 (July 21, 1994) 157, 159-64, at 162.

Homily 14

1. For this background I am indebted to William Barclay, *The Gospel of Matthew* 2 (rev. ed.; Philadelphia: Westminster, 1975) 193.

2. The Greek could also mean "70 times seven times," i.e. 490 times; see Daniel J. Harrington, *The Gospel of Matthew* (Sacra pagina 1; Collegeville, Minn.: Liturgical, 1991) 269.

3. I have dealt with this problem in somewhat different fashion in a homily at the University of Notre Dame in 1984; see "A Brother Whom I Have Pardoned," in my collection *Grace on Crutches: Homilies for Fellow Travelers* (New York/Mahwah: Paulist, 1986) 118-23.

4. Reference to a recent incident in New York City that captured the imagination of Americans, mainly because of the captive's incredible ability to preserve his sanity in a terribly restricted "cage" below ground.

5. See Harrington, *The Gospel of Matthew* 269.

6. Patrick J. Ryan, "Crime and Sin," *America* 169, no. 5 (Aug. 28, 1993) 31.

7. I borrow this from an account from Rome by Andrew Nagorski in *Newsweek*, Jan. 7, 1985, 25.

8. For this insight I an indebted to Robert J. Schreiter, *Reconciliation: Mission and Ministry in a Changing Social Order* (Maryknoll, N.Y./Cambridge, Mass.: Orbis/Boston Theological Institute, 1992) 44-46.

Homily 15

1. This homily was preached during the Preaching the Just Word retreat/workshop for priests and other ministers of the Diocese of Paterson, N.J.

2. See Joseph A. Fitzmyer, S.J., *Paul and His Theology: A Brief Sketch* (2nd ed.; Englewood Cliffs, N.J.: Prentice Hall, 1989) 94, no. 130. Also Jerome Murphy-O'Connor, O.P., "The First Letter to the Corinthians," *The New Jerome Biblical Commentary* (Englewood Cliffs, N.J.: Prentice Hall, 1990) 49:56, p. 809.

Homily 16

1. This homily was delivered to priests of the Dioceses of Oakland, Sacramento, and San Jose, within my project Preaching the Just Word, at San Damiano Retreat Center, Danville, California.
2. See Joseph A. Fitzmyer, S.J., *The Gospel according to Luke (I-IX)* (Garden City, N.Y.: Doubleday, 1981) 712-13.
3. Ibid. 712.
4. Ibid.

Homily 17

1. A new TV series, set in a Chicago hospital.
2. A reference to a strike that forced the cancellation of regular-season games, playoffs, and the World Series in 1994.
3. See D. J. McCarthy, "Prophecy (in the Bible)," *New Catholic Encyclopedia* 11 (1967) 861.
4. See Abraham J. Heschel, *The Prophets* (New York: Harper & Row, 1962) 24: "In the presence of God [the Hebrew prophet] takes the part of the people. In the presence of the people he takes the part of God."
5. See Conrad E. L'Heureux, "Numbers," *The New Jerome Biblical Commentary*, ed. Raymond E. Brown, S.S., Joseph A. Fitzmyer, S.J., and Roland E. Murphy, O.Carm. (Englewood Cliffs, N.J.: Prentice Hall, 1990) 5:27, p. 85.
6. Here I am borrowing the engaging rhetoric of Marian Burkhart (no nepotism here) in her article "In the Paraclete I Trust: Women, the Priesthood, & the Patriarchy," *Commonweal* 121, no. 9 (May 6, 1994) 15-16, at 16.
7. Vatican II, Dogmatic Constitution on the Church, no. 12.
8. William J. O'Malley, "The Goldilocks Method," *America* 165, no. 14 (Nov. 9, 1991) 334-39, at 336.
9. Origen, *Homily on the Book of Judges* 2.3.
10. For a more extended treatment of this facet of Jesus' teaching, see my homily "Cut It Off?" in my collection *Lovely in Eyes Not His: Homilies for an Imaging of Christ* (New York/Mahwah: Paulist, 1988) 98-103.
11. Another possible approach to this passage is suggested by Daniel J. Harrington, S.J., "The Gospel according to Mark," *The New Jerome Biblical Commentary* (n. 5 above) 41:61, p. 617: "That these sayings had a communal dimension and served to exclude members of the church who gave offense is plausible in view of ancient Greco-Roman uses of the body as a communal metaphor."

Homily 18

1. This homily was delivered to priests of the Diocese of Portland, Maine, during my retreat/workshop Preaching the Just Word.

2. See T. A. Caldwell, "Samaritans," *New Catholic Encyclopedia* 12 (1967) 1009-1010.

3. Robert J. Karris, O.F.M., "The Gospel according to Luke," *The New Jerome Biblical Commentary*, ed. Raymond E. Brown, S.S., Joseph A. Fitzmyer, S.J., and Roland E. Murphy, O.Carm. (Englewood Cliffs, N.J.: Prentice Hall, 1990) 43:126, p. 702.

Homily 19

1. John Carmody, "When People's Concerns Meet Jesus Christ, Church Lives," *National Catholic Reporter* 29, no. 42 (Oct. 1, 1993) 2.

2. This homily was delivered during a Preaching the Just Word retreat/workshop for priests gathered from various sections of the United States; hence the focus on justice and its proclamation.

3. See F. Schroeder, "Paul, Apostle, St.," *New Catholic Encyclopedia* 11 (1967) 1-12, at 8. "This description, found in the apocryphal *Acts of Paul*, derives from the legend of Paul and Thecla and is unflattering enough to be authentic..." (ibid.).

4. See 1 Cor 7:22; Gal 1:10; Phil 1:1; 2:22; also Joseph A. Fitzmyer, S.J., "The Letter to the Romans," *The New Jerome Biblical Commentary*, ed. Raymond E. Brown, S.S., Joseph A. Fitzmyer, S.J., and Roland E. Murphy, O.Carm. (Englewood Cliffs, N.J.: Prentice Hall, 1990) 51:15, p. 833.

5. See Joseph A. Fitzmyer, S.J., *Paul and His Theology: A Brief Sketch* (Englewood Cliffs, N.J.: Prentice Hall, 1989) 36 ff.

6. Robert J. Karris, O.F.M., "The Gospel according to Luke," *The New Jerome Biblical Commentary* (n. 4 above) 43:131, p. 703.

7. Joseph A. Fitzmyer, S.J., *The Gospel according to Luke (X-XXIV)* (Garden City, N.Y.: Doubleday, 1985) 935.

8. See the English translation in *The Pope Speaks* 21, no. 1 (spring 1976) 1-51.

9. *Evangelii nuntiandi* 22 (*The Pope Speaks* 14).

10. Ibid. 27 (*The Pope Speaks* 16).

11. Ibid. 29 (*The Pope Speaks* 17).

12. Ibid. 30 (*The Pope Speaks* 18). Here Paul is speaking specifically of the peoples of the Third World.

13. Ibid. 36 (*The Pope Speaks* 20).

14. Ibid. 34 (*The Pope Speaks* 19).

15. Ibid. 36 (*The Pope Speaks* 20).

16. Carmody, n. 1 above.

Homily 20

1. In a message (September 1990) to the World Summit for Children, quoted in an editorial by Anthony J. Schulte, O.F.M., "Make Room in the

Inn for the World's Children," *St. Anthony Messenger* 98, no. 7 (December 1990) 26.

2.   Quoted ibid.

Homily 21

1.   Christopher John Farley, "Rock's Anxious Rebels," *Time* 142, no. 17 (Oct. 25, 1993) 60-66.
2.   This homily was delivered at a retreat/workshop within my project Preaching the Just Word, for priests of dioceses in Louisiana.
3.   A reference to a popular soap opera.
4.   So Joseph A. Fitzmyer, S.J., *The Gospel according to Luke (X-XXIV)* (Garden City, N.Y.: Doubleday, 1985) 1013.
5.   Ibid. 1011.
6.   Augustine, *First Catechetical Instruction* 1.4.7 (tr. Ancient Christian Writers 2, 21).
7.   Second Vatican Council, Constitution on the Church in the Modern World, no. 1.

Homily 22

1.   John O'Donnell, S.J., "Faith," *The New Dictionary of Theology*, ed. Joseph A. Komonchak, Mary Collins, and Dermot A. Lane (Wilmington, Del.: Michael Glazier, 1987) 375-86, at 377. Here O'Donnell is summarizing Hans Urs von Balthasar, "Fides Christi," in *Sponsa Verbi: Skizzen zur Theologie* 2 (Einsiedeln: Johannes, 1961) 45-79.
2.   Karl Rahner, "Following the Crucified," *Theological Investigations* 18: *God and Revelation* (New York: Crossroad, 1983) 157-70, at 165-66.
3.   This homily was preached to priests of the Diocese of Winona, Minnesota, as part of the retreat/workshop that is my project Preaching the Just Word.
4.   Second Vatican Council, Decree on the Ministry and Life of Priests, no. 4. Since Latin does not have a definite or an indefinite article, it is not clear whether the council was listing proclamation of the gospel as *the* primary duty or *a* primary duty of a priest.

Homily 23

1.   See Roland E. Murphy, O.Carm., "Canticle of Canticles," in *The New Jerome Biblical Commentary*, ed. Raymond E. Brown, S.S., Joseph A. Fitzmyer, S.J., and Roland E. Murphy, O.Carm. (Englewood Cliffs, N.J.: Prentice Hall, 1990) 29:6-8, p. 463.
2.   See ibid. 29:24, p. 465.
3.   See their booklet *Children and Families First* (Washington, D.C.: United States Catholic Conference, 1992).
4.   In a message (September 1990) to the World Summit for Children,

quoted in an editorial by Anthony J. Schulte, O.F.M., "Make Room in the Inn for the World's Children," *St. Anthony Messenger* 98, no. 7 (December 1990) 26.

5. See Mary Rose McGeady, *God's Lost Children: Letters from Covenant House* (New York: Covenant House, 1991) 31; Ruth Leger Sivard, *World Military and Social Expenditures: 1991* (14th ed.; Washington, D.C.: World Priorities, 1991) 48; [U.S. Catholic Conference,] *Children and Families First: A Catholic Campaign* (Washington, D.C.: United States Catholic Conference, 1992) 10.

6. McGeady, *God's Lost Children*, Dedication.

Homily 24

1. I say "suggest" because I do not say that my presentation is the literal meaning of the texts; they do apply, however, to the situation of marriage.

2. From the introduction to Tobit in *The Oxford Annotated Bible with the Apocrypha: Revised Standard Version*, ed. Herbert G. May and Bruce M. Metzger (New York: Oxford University, 1965) [63]. Here Tobit is placed among the Apocrypha.

3. Mary Jordan's article was headed "In Cities Like Atlanta, Whites Are Passing on Public Schools"; Kevin Sullivan's, "Persevering, Breath by Breath."

4. See Kevin Sullivan, "On Thin Ice," *Washington Post Magazine*, Feb. 7, 1993, 12-15, 17-30.

5. Marian Williamson, *Return to Love* (New York: HarperCollins, 1992).

6. "Sister Act" is a reference to a delightful film starring Whoopi Goldberg.

Homily 25

1. *Time* 141, no. 25 (June 21, 1993) 67-68.

2. The enrollment at Marquette University in the fall of 1986.

3. See Evelyn Whitehead and James D. Whitehead, "Christian Marriage," *U.S. Catholic* 47, no. 6 (June 1982) 9.

4. A reference to the final game in World Cup soccer 1994, with Brazil registering an unprecedented fourth title, 1-0.

Homily 27

1. This homily was delivered at the Eucharist which closed the five-day Preaching the Just Word retreat/workshop for the priests of the Archdiocese of Dubuque, June 19-24, 1994.

2. John Kohan, "A Voice in the Wilderness," *Time* 143, no. 25 (June 20, 1994) 46-47, at 46.

3. Ibid. 47.

4. Paul VI, apostolic exhortation *Evangelization in the Modern World* (Dec. 8, 1975) nos. 29, 34, 36.

Homily 28

1. This homily was delivered to priests of the Diocese of Des Moines, Iowa, during a five-day retreat/workshop in my program Preaching the Just Word.
2. For biographical information, I am indebted especially to Henri Daniel-Rops, *Monsieur Vincent: The Story of St. Vincent de Paul* (New York: Hawthorn, 1961), and Mary Purcell, *The World of Monsieur Vincent* (Chicago: Loyola University, 1989; "a newly revised edition" of the original published by Harvill in London and Scribner's in New York in 1963).
3. Daniel-Rops, *Monsieur Vincent* 17.
4. Purcell, *The World of Monsieur Vincent* 40-41.
5. Quoted in Purcell, ibid. 66.
6. Quoted by Daniel-Rops, *Monsieur Vincent* 59.
7. Ibid. 94.
8. Ibid. 111-12.
9. Quoted ibid. 99.
10. Quoted from J. Calvet by Purcell, *The World of Monsieur Vincent* 101.
11. Quoted by Purcell, ibid. 108.
12. Quoted by Purcell, ibid. 210.
13. Quoted by Daniel-Rops, *Monsieur Vincent* 12.
14. Walter Brueggemann, "The Preacher, the Text, and the People," *Theology Today* 47 (1990) 237-47, at 237.
15. Constitution on the Church in the Modern World, no. 24.
16. Ibid., no. 32.
17. See Roland E. Murphy, O.Carm., "Canticle of Canticles," in *The New Jerome Biblical Commentary*, ed. Raymond E. Brown, S.S., Joseph A. Fitzmyer, S.J., and Roland E. Murphy, O.Carm. (Englewood Cliffs, N.J.: Prentice Hall, 1990) 29:24, p. 465.

Homily 29

1. This homily was composed for a liturgy shared by the Jesuit community of St. Aloysius Gonzaga in Washington, D.C., commemorating the feast of St. Alphonsus Rodriguez.
2. For the information in this second point, I am largely indebted to Joseph N. Tylenda, S.J., *Jesuit Saints & Martyrs: Short Biographies of the Saints, Blessed, Venerables, and Servants of God of the Society of Jesus* (Chicago: Loyola University, 1984) 379-81.
3. See W. Yeomans, S.J., *St Alphonsus Rodriguez: Autobiography* (London: Chapman, 1964) 242.
4. I am aware that in this meditation Ignatius speaks explicitly of "God,"

not of Christ. But, as Hugo Rahner states emphatically, "In full accordance with Ignatian theology, the 'creator and Lord' of this contemplation is Christ, the incarnate Word, who in virtue of what he is and of what he does, dwells in all creatures and 'behaves as one who works'..." (*Ignatius the Theologian* [New York: Herder and Herder, 1968] 134).

Homily 30

1. This homily was preached on a day when the Shrine of the Sacred Heart in Baltimore, Maryland, brought to a close its celebration of its 125th anniversary and dedicated its new organ.
2. Gregory Dix, *The Shape of the Liturgy* (Westminster, Eng.: Dacre, 1945) 744.
3. St. Thomas Aquinas, *Adoro te*, in the translation of Gerard Manley Hopkins, *S. Thomae Aquinatis Rhythmus ad SS. Sacramentum*, in W. H. Gardner and N. H. MacKenzie, *The Poems of Gerard Manley Hopkins* (4th ed.; New York: Oxford University, 1970) 211.
4. I have developed these ideas more fully in my homily "Sing a New Song to the Lord," published in my *Dare To Be Christ: Homilies for the Nineties* (New York/Mahwah: Paulist, 1990) 190-95. The present homily uses some different illustrations.
5. Constitution on the Sacred Liturgy, no. 112.
6. Ibid., no. 120. I regret that the council speaks explicitly of "minds" (*mentes*) only; see my own next paragraph.
7. I am convinced that in this text the Greek word *kardia* stresses the emotional side of the human person, filling out an aspect of loving not as clear in "soul" and "mind." See the treatment of *kardia* in William F. Arndt and F. Wilbur Gingrich, *A Greek-English Lexicon of the New Testament and Other Early Christian Literature* (Chicago: Univ. of Chicago, 1957) 404-5.

Homily 31

1. I have this from Bernie S. Siegel, M.D., *Love, Medicine & Miracles* (New York: Harper & Row, 1988) 2.
2. Quoted by Alain K. Laing, "Hippocrates," *World Book Encyclopedia* 9 (1975) 227.
3. Siegel xii.
4. This homily was delivered to the 1993 graduating class of the Georgetown University School of Medicine.
5. For detailed information see the material gathered by Richard G. Brown, "The Griefs and Anxieties of This Age" (2nd ed., 1993), and privately printed by the Woodstock Theological Center, Georgetown University, Washington, D.C.
6. See Louis S. Richman, "Struggling To Save Our Kids," *Fortune* 126, no. 3 (Aug. 10, 1992) 34-40.

7.   David Rogers, M.D., "The Special Case of AIDS in Public Health," in Kevin M. Cahill, M.D., ed., *Imminent Peril: Public Health in a Declining Economy* (New York: Twentieth Century Fund, 1991) 57-63, at 62 (italics in text).

8.   Ibid. 34.

9.   Mario M. Cuomo, "Public Health: Old Truth, New Realities," in Cahill, *Imminent Peril* 123-36, at 126.

10. Ibid. 127-28.

11. Richard Selzer, *Mortal Lessons: Notes on the Art of Surgery* (New York: Simon and Schuster, 1976) 46, 48.

12. Siegel, *Love, Medicine & Miracles* 181.

13. Ibid. 66.

14. George Annas, as quoted by Nancy Gibbs, "R$_x$ for Death," *Time* 141, no. 22 (May 31, 1993) 34-39, at 36.

15. A reference to the doctor who has made death-assisted suicide his specialty.

16. Siegel, *Love, Medicine & Miracles* xii (italics mine).

17. Quoted by William F. Buckley Jr. in a syndicated column I found in the *Stuart News* (Florida) of April 10, 1993, A17. The judge is Edwin Torres.

Homily 32

1.   The occasion was the graduation Mass for the 1994 class of the Georgetown University Medical Center, Washington, D.C.

2.   See the uncommonly moving book *Compassion: A Reflection on the Christian Life* by Donald P. McNeill, Douglas A. Morrison, and Henri J. M. Nouwen (Garden City, N.Y.: Doubleday, 1982) 3-9.

3.   Quoted ibid. 6.

4.   From the manuscript graciously supplied me by the author, H. Logan Holtgrewe, M.D., "Our Nation's Health Care Dilemma—Who Pays? How Do We Pay? What Can We Afford?" 11. The bioethicist quoted is Steven G. Post, "Health Care Rationing," *America*, Nov. 18, 1992.

5.   From Bernie S. Siegel, M.D., *Love, Medicine & Miracles* (New York: Harper & Row, 1988) 183.

6.   Frederick Buechner, *The Magnificent Defeat* (New York: Seabury, 1966) 23.

Homily 33

1.   These reflections were presented during a Christmas songfest that involved the Georgetown Community Chorale, the Saint Aloysius Gospel Choir, and the Gonzaga Liturgical Chamber Ensemble.

2.   *Nestorii sermo* (ed. E. Schwartz, *Acta conciliorum oecumenicorum* 1.5.1.30); *Nestorius, Liber Heraclidis* 2.1 (tr. F. Nau et al., *Le Livre d'Héraclide de Damas* [Paris, 1910] 176); *Nestorii tractatus* (ACO 1.5.1.38).

3. Boston: Beacon, 1994. Much of the information that follows stems from this volume.
4. Marian Wright Edelman, ibid. xvii.
5. See ibid.
6. Ibid.
7. See Pol Castel, "Looking for the Way Together in Jewish-Christian Dialogue," *America* 171, no. 19 (Dec. 17-24, 1994) 12-15, 18-20, at 20.